SUCCEEDING AT SAAS:

COMPUTING IN THE CLOUD

AMY D. WOHL

Published by Wohl Associates

Copyright © October 2008 Amy D. Wohl

ISBN 978-0-615-25636-8

INTRODUCTION

Software as a Service (SaaS) is not a new idea, but rather a new name for a concept that crops up at intervals, each time strengthened by technology that is better suited to provide its features, technologists who have a better understanding of what customers require and what the market will require for financial success, and customers who are better educated as to what the concept can offer them.

It is a method of providing and distributing the functionality of software that permits an individual or an organization to benefit from its use without taking on its implementation or ongoing management. This means it can often be used more quickly, at lesser expense, and by individuals and organizations without the internal resources to implement and support complex, modern software and systems.

SaaS is offered by a dazzling array of potential players. They include traditional software vendors (ISVs) moving to the web, new net-native software vendors building their business on the SaaS models, and a variety of platform players who offer an infrastructure on which ISVs can host and market their software. Some platform players are interested in creating an ecosystem around applications or infrastructure tools of their own; others are interested in providing aggregation and marketing as a service.

From the end-user's point of view, SaaS may also be offered by resellers, offering ISVs or platform players branded solutions (with or without their own solutions and services added into the value proposition) and by huge hosting organizations with vast customer bases of their own such as ISPs (web hosters) and telcos (Telephone companies).

In the future, SaaS may also be offered as part of services such as banking, financial services (investments, retirement, etc.), healthcare, or e-commerce, vanishing entirely into the service, and not recognized as "software" at all.

Today, perhaps half of business organizations are using at least one SaaS application and more than half of non-users are considering SaaS. Many research firms believe that by 2010-20012 about 25-30% of all new software will be delivered on SaaS platforms. That means a substantial amount of software will move to this new technology and a substantial number of buyers will buy some (but probably not all) of their software using SaaS. Keep in mind that some software will be deemed too valuable or too risky (in need of high levels of security) to go outside of company control; other software will simply not be possible or economically justifiable to rewrite to the new platform.

For small, new firms and individual consumers SaaS may represent a more compelling solution, and much higher percentages of usage may be found in these markets.

The SaaS market started out as a complement to the traditional software market. Many existing vendors thought of it as a way to sell a "tweaked" version of their existing software to smaller firms it had previously been too expensive to market to or support. Software start-up firms entering the SaaS market, of course, built software optimized for delivery on the SaaS platform. Some initially also targeted the SMB market, but others focused on the enterprise market from the start. In any case, large enterprises (those with more than a few thousand employees) have looked at SaaS for at least some applications from the start. Financial services, professional services, and retail firms have been particularly aggressive in adopting the SaaS model.

We are still at the beginning of the SaaS market. The larger players (Microsoft, IBM, Oracle, and Adobe) are now entering into the market as well as Telcos and ISPs of every size, all over the world. New forms of SaaS vendors (platform providers, aggregators, integrators) are coming into the mainstream. New applications of every kind are coming on line. And large enterprises have the choice of building their own SaaS architecture internally to take advantage of the efficiency, speed and flexibility of SaaS, while maintaining the control and security they may require.

Steve Mills, Executive Vice President in charge of IBM's $20 billion software business, believes that SaaS is really a service business and that there are a lot of services already being delivered that we are not yet counting, such as ADP and other payroll services, as well as airline and entertainment ticketing services – a huge market. We'd agree, noting that it is this market where the software disappears inside the service it provides. That will be the big business opportunity in the future.

The game has only just begun.[1] It is changing so quickly that we were unwilling to use conventional publishing for this book. By using an electronic publishing process, we can be in print just four weeks after I write my last word, and make revisions to the book whenever we choose (probably in six months). This seems appropriate for a subject that is so dynamic that it changes even as we try to understand it.

---

[1]According to a study by *Rackspace*, a hosting company, performed in March 2007,

- Fifty-one percent of respondents already use a SaaS application and 72 percent of those SaaS users are considering additional SaaS applications.
- Sixty-nine percent of respondents see SaaS as the preferred software delivery method of the future.
- Thirty-four percent of respondents that are not currently using a SaaS application are considering it.

The 420 participants (of 2788 queried) in the survey were RackSpace customers and varied in size from firms with annual revenue from $1 million to $1 billion.

Table of Contents

Description   **Page**

Introduction iii

SECTION I: ISSUES FOR EVERYONE *9*

What is Software as a Service? 10

Nothing's New: SaaS's Historical Precedents 12

What's Different This Time? 15

SECTION II: ISSUES FOR VENDORS *19*

Chapter 1. **The Software Market Today and Tomorrow**.... **20**

How Does the SaaS Market Work? 20

How is SaaS Different than Traditional Software? 36

Chapter 2. **Making the SaaS Decision** **40**

Deciding to Participate 40

The Opportunity 40

The Competition 45

Making Good Decisions to Assure SaaS Success 49

Chapter 3. **Planning for Success in SaaS** **51**

The New Business Model 51

Planning the New Financial Model 51

Sales and Marketing 53

Marketing Costs 53

A Different Distribution Model Needs a Different Sales Plan .. 57

Product Design 63

A Different Model can Lead to Different Products 63

Chapter 4. The Economic Life Cycle of Software Applications .67

Is Customization Supportable? 69

The Relationship between SaaS and SOA 71

Chapter 5. The Cost of Changing to SaaS 74

Rewriting or Porting the Application 74

Changing the Business Model 75

Changing Sources of Revenue 76

Changes in Operational Costs 77

Other Migration Costs...79

Cost of a Hybrid Business Model 80

Chapter 6. Pricing 83

How to Price for SaaS...83

Billing...87

SECTION III: ISSUES FOR CUSTOMERS................................ 91

Chapter 7. Customer Expectations.....................................92

Who Uses SaaS? 92

What do Customers Want?..94

Chapter 8. **Challenges and Choices** 99

Integration 99

Customization 101

Picking the Right Vendor...101

Standards 102

SECTION IV: THE FUTURE OF SAAS................................. 103

Chapter 9. **Customer Trends**.. 105

Customer Expectations..105

Bringing SaaS In-House 110

Chapter 10. **Technology Trends** 116

Cloud Computing 116

The Convergence of SaaS and SOA 118

SECTION V: CONCLUSIONS.. 119

ISSUES FOR EVERYONE

In this book, we'll be looking at issues that affect the SaaS community as a whole, issues for ISVs looking to become SaaS vendors, and issues for customers who want to buy software in the SaaS marketplace. To make it easier for everyone, the book is divided into sections so you can focus on the parts that are most relevant to your interests. Of course, we hope you'll choose to read it all! I particularly urge you to read this section on **Issues for Everyone** first, since it provides some definitions and background – and unless you're like me and read books back-to-front, you might consider saving the *Future of SaaS* section for last. It's dessert.

What is Software as a Service?

SaaS is simply software which is delivered from a server in a remote location to your desktop, and is used on-line. Typically, it is used via a browser interface, although some SaaS software uses its own interface, designed to provide special characteristics for its application or its users. Initially, SaaS software existed only in real time, within an on-line connection; when the connection was interrupted, the user had no data and no application.

As SaaS evolved, the on-line-only model remains as the predominant model, but it has been joined by SaaS applications which live on an appliance (a server managed by the SaaS vendor) on the user organization's premises, as well as by other SaaS applications which place interfaces, applications, and data on users desktops and mobile devices (laptops, smartphones), synching them to the on-line versions to keep everything up-to-date. This allows users to work without interruption, whether they have an Internet connection available or not, and to handle airplane rides, black holes in the network, and network failures (mine are mainly due to my ISP, but some users find theirs are mainly due to their SaaS provider's software).

Some do not take the notion of parking their data or applications on a server they do not control and cannot physically touch or see lightly.

Some IT professionals believe SaaS is not mature enough for any but the most casual usage, often citing variable and unreliable performance and the possibility of lost or corrupted data. We'd note that the best SaaS providers (and why would you use anyone else?) use professional data centers, provisioned and staffed beyond the resources of all but the largest enterprises. Data that is too valuable to risk should either not be exposed to web-based storage or should be backed up on your own premises as well as on the web. Good practices don't change because a new method of software distribution becomes available.

> **SaaS is a fundamental change in the software market and a strong disruptive force**

SaaS is a fundamental change in the software market and a strong disruptive force.

- It empowers users to select software and implement it without having to wait for IT to find the time and resources to provision them. It offers a new concept of Time to Value that can be compelling for marketing departments, product developers, and others in a rush to get something begun.

- It permits small companies, with little or no internal IT, to have access to the same applications that were previously available to only the largest enterprises. Just as the spreadsheet made data and the ability to manipulate it available to any company, SaaS makes sophisticated data analysis and management tools available to companies of any size.

- It offers an opportunity for a new generation of software companies, exploiting the Internet as their platform, to challenge the current incumbents, who must decide whether to defend their turf or divide their resources between supporting and marketing existing applications on traditional platforms and trying to build and market SaaS applications which have a different design philosophy and may require different marketing plans.

Nothing's New: SaaS's Historical Precedents

Ancient History – Time Shared Computing

Nothing is new – and neither is the idea of using software from a remote, managed location. In the seventies, this was called time-shared computing. It was expensive and not very flexible because in the pre-Internet era, accessing a remote server meant implementing a private data network. This was a decision not taken lightly and a game mainly for large companies trying to offer their locations access to the same software or to collect data (such as daily sales) promptly. Adding a piece of hardware or a new application to the environment was difficult, time-consuming, and expensive. These networks often used whatever they had for long periods of time because the change process was so daunting. Integration across applications from multiple software vendors was a task for highly-skilled (and very expensive) Systems Integrators, typically adding to their specific knowledge on the customer's dime. Custom code could be unpredictable.

The ASP Market, the Dot.com Bubble, and Why it didn't Work

The Internet changed all that. Suddenly, there was a ubiquitous, standard interconnection mechanism. Anyone, anywhere could be connected or disconnected easily. With a little work, we could make them secure. Quickly, developers realized there was an opportunity to offer access to software applications over the Internet. The ASP round was on.

ASP Type	Service	Customer
ASP SW Aggregator	Provides Internet access to (popular) SW	Individual Professionals; SMB
Traditional ISV	Adapts his own SW to Internet with minor changes; provides hosting	SMB
Net-Native ISV	Writes new SW for the Internet	Consumers to Mid-market Enterprises

By 1998, hundreds of companies decided that they could acquire licenses to existing software, host it for access via the Internet, and be an ASP (Application Services Provider). A much smaller number set out to build software that would take advantage of being "net native" – built to run across the Internet and exploit it.

But the ASP round didn't last. Most of the early ASPs were unsuccessful. Some ended up as part of a few larger firms. Many simply disappeared. The players, however, noted what hadn't worked and continued, many turning up in other startups or joining firms that survived the Internet Bubble.

The mistakes in the late 90's and at the turn of the 21st

century were readily identifiable in retrospect.

1. Products based on Technology Bets, Not User Needs: Early ASP's were either existing ISVs or new startups. Most of them entered the on-line market because they believed they had a "good" application, not based on interaction with users (via focus groups, user observation in usability labs, or trial usage) to assure that the software they were building was something users actually wanted and needed, offered in a form users could readily consume. They took the view that if they built good technology it would attract customers. This supply-side view of the demand for technology rarely works today (although we still see developers offering products based on this model).

2. Few Business Models: Most ASPs had no business models. They "priced to the market," frequently not charging enough to cover their costs, or pricing valuable services well below what customers might be willing to pay for unique or convenient services. Many had no idea how they would actually make money – they just assumed they would.

3. A New Distribution Channel via the Internet: Many of the original ASP's were ISVs looking for a new way to get their software to market. Typically they were technologically astute, but knew little about marketing. Everyone thought that simply making applications available on the magical Internet would be enough; users would find them through word of mouth – viral marketing. These ISVs rarely built marketing plans into their business models, nor did they allocate marketing budgets. Unfortunately, while on-line software has many benefits, customers must still be sold, and marketing to create product awareness and brand recognition is vital.

4. Data Center Distractions: In the beginning, almost every

ISV thought it was important to build and control his own data center. This meant significant capital investments and large budgets for technical staff. Also, the ISV either had to start with a very small data center (a server in the back room wasn't unusual), hoping to add to it as customers arrived, or to bet on the future with a very large data center, requiring a major financial investment. In the first case, the ISV and its customers were vulnerable to unacceptable performance during peak periods and downtime caused by unscheduled failures; in the second case, the ISV (and his investors) had to bear the high cost of a large data center that was rarely used to its capacity.

5. Educating a New Market: The market was completely uneducated as to the value of on-line application software and its infrastructure. It would take several years of education, examples, and success to educate the market. In 1999, we performed a primary market research study on the ASP market,[2] interviewing 100 ASP vendors (mainly ISVs) and 100 potential customers (half large enterprises, half smaller ones). Only a small percentage of the large enterprises knew much about the ASP model; almost none of the smaller ones did.

What's Different This Time?

All of these mistakes have been corrected in the SaaS round.

1. **Market Requirements:** Most SaaS vendors have gotten much better at listening to potential buyers. Applications are written with user requirements in mind. New SaaS applications attempt to match what the best application in their category offers and then go on to provide more – a better interface, better integration with other applications, more features (especially web features).

---

[2] Assessing the ASP Opportunity, Wohl Associates, 2000

2. **Stronger Business Models:** While there is still a lot of room for improvement in SaaS vendors' business models, they've come a long way from the ASPs of the late nineties, when there might be no real business model at all.

    Today, most SaaS vendors plan to monetize their software (or the 3rd party software they license for distribution) by either making a charge for each user or each transaction (rarer) or by using an **advertising** model where the user is exposed to presumably relevant ads in exchange for access to the software.

    Sometimes the two techniques are combined: ads are used to support a trial usage period and then the user is invited to switch to a premium service (no ads), with better support, more features, and a subscription fee.

    For business applications and larger customers in the mid-market and the enterprise (as opposed to the consumer and SOHO market), SaaS vendors go straight to a subscription basis, often with a multi-year commitment.

3. **Better Financing:** SaaS is now a respectable business that has an excellent chance of generating positive cash flows and profits. In some cases, it has also permitted successful IPOs and mergers and acquisitions, all providing profitable exit strategies for investors. With the popularity of SaaS, venture capitalists have swarmed into this market, investing in company after company, often on terms which would have seemed lavish a few years ago. Not only do investors bring money for additional development and more substantial marketing investments, they also bring their networks of contacts, offering new arrays and access to both partners and customers. They also bring more seasoned management skills, so they can mentor SaaS start-ups or nudge them into hiring more appropriate management as their companies grow in size and

sophistication.

4. **Market Focus:** Almost all the original ASP vendors thought they were in the SMB business. Some of them still are, selling largely to companies with 5 to 200 users and 20 to 500 employees. Others are selling all over the demographic game, from Very Small Businesses with fewer than 5 employees, to large Enterprises with thousands. A few packages are useful to everyone, regardless of size; most are not. In fact, most SaaS vendors attempt to focus on a particular part of the marketplace, generally based on the skills sets of their existing staff. They may choose a company size to focus on or they may prefer to specialize in one or more vertical markets such as insurance, healthcare, or local government. Often they pick both. Companies outside their selected demographic may find them and choose to become customers, but they are usually not actively marketing to multiple demographics unless they have multiple product and marketing strategies (like Salesforce.com and Intacct).

5. **Outsourcing for Outsourcers:** Between the ASP round and the SaaS round, most of the ISVs discovered that it was better to partner for infrastructure than to invest in and run it yourself. This decision was assisted by the rise of a new layer of players who were interested in providing infrastructure (compute power, storage, systems management, perhaps billing) for SaaS, but not SaaS applications and generally not marketing.

    These new SaaS data center providers are not all alike. We shall look at quite a few of them. Platform as a Service (PaaS) providers like OpSource provide hosting, billing, and some marketing and support. Salesforce.com is both a successful SaaS ISV and a PaaS provider who has built an ecosystem of partners who write not just on their platform but on top of their application as well. JamCracker is both a PaaS provider and an Aggregator who sells selected ISVs' applications, providing cross-application integration, support, and marketing.

6. **A Better Educated Market:** While the ISVs were moving toward net-native applications and the market was moving toward a partnership approach with ISVs partnered with PaaS providers, the users were experimenting with SaaS. They found that it could offer them access to applications much more quickly than the traditional decision and implementation process. Decisions could be made quickly because there were few up-front fees to pay and SaaS was treated as an expense rather than a capital expenditure. Many applications could be accessed within hours or days, rather than the months it could take to prepare a traditional software application.

Often, although ISVs expected their SaaS applications to be used mainly by SMBs, they found that individuals and departments in enterprises were users, too, attracted by the easy access and ease of use. Both word of mouth and better use of formal marketing spread the word, leading to significant success for some vendors. Several vendors have more than a million users and Salesforce has more than $1 Billion in revenue (2008). Success, of course, leads to more interest, attracting additional users to the market. It is estimated that about 70% of companies will use SaaS within the next few years and more than 25% of new software will be delivered via SaaS (IDC).

ISSUES FOR VENDORS

Chapter 1. The Software Market Today and Tomorrow

How Does the SaaS Market Work?

SaaS isn't really a product in itself, but rather a combination of a product (software) and its distribution mechanism. In the marketplace, a SaaS offering competes with other software products (both SaaS and traditional software offerings) and may find itself being distributed in a number of different ways.

Software creators: In the beginning, many SaaS products were offered by their developers, so typically each product was being offered by its own ISV (and on its own infrastructure). The ISV was entirely responsible for its marketing and support. With their focus on technical skills and non-marketing orientation, this didn't work very well.

Market creators rather than Software creators: From the beginning, some SaaS vendors (some of the original ASPs), were not software developers, but rather resellers. They made arrangements with ISVs to license and resell their software on a SaaS platform. Typically, very little adaption of the software from a traditional platform to the new SaaS environment was attempted and marketing efforts were minimal. Support was often minimal, too; these early SaaS resellers hadn't thought about their business model and often had difficulty staying afloat.

As some players removed themselves from the market entirely, others pulled back and rethought their options. From these early experiments, new models for how the SaaS market might work emerged. When the second round began, c. 2005, the players were prepared to arrange themselves differently.

We still had software creators (ISVs or developers), but they now tended to focus on the software. Often they partnered with a platform provider (PaaS) for the infrastructure they might require. That platform provider might also offer marketing assistance or access to customers and markets.

Other platform providers became **Aggregators,** actively seeking out software creators whose products they could sell to their own customers on an exclusive or non-exclusive basis. These customers could be single companies of any size but they could also be business partners who would then resell the aggregators' portfolio products to their own customers, who might number in the thousands or even millions. These customers were often telephone companies (telcos), financial institutions, or other companies with large numbers of customers with whom they had existing service relationships. Often the products were custom branded not with the aggregator's brand, but rather with his customer's brand, making the product appear friendly and familiar to a consumer who was far removed from the ISV and the software market. In some cases, it isn't clear that the ultimate customer is thinking about buying software at all, but rather about using a branded service.

Revenue flows in these multi-tier relationships can be substantial in total, but tiny for any transaction. The telco may be collecting only a few dollars a month from his customer (or a few cents per transaction). He will probably pay a percentage of his revenue (perhaps against a minimum) to the aggregator who then pays a fee (fixed or variable) to the ISV. The software might be running on the aggregator's infrastructure, supported by his team, or running on his customer's infrastructure, depending on their business arrangements, and who has the IT capacity and resources available. Remember that while a few cents a transaction seems like not much, multiplied by millions of customers and even a dozen transactions per customer per month it can be substantial.

ISVs strive to build ecosystems of partners who will build applications around their application, making it more valuable and "sticky." Some of these applications will be built for individual customers. Others will be built as custom solutions but will then be offered as generalized solutions in the marketplace (systems integrators and consultants often do this as a portfolio of intellectual property can greatly extend the value of their human capital). Some applications will simply be built to be offered to the marketplace.

In addition to ISVs and Aggregators, you will see other players in the SaaS marketplace. A player like **Microsoft** is in many categories.

Microsoft is such an overwhelming presence in the software market that it's almost remarkable to realize that they have a much smaller influence to date over the SaaS market. But Microsoft is not ignoring SaaS; they are just trying to fit it into an overall strategy that is different than most other companies. When you start from a point of view where you are the dominant player in two important markets – operating systems and office productivity software – your outlook on everything is likely to be different.

For example, Microsoft has long looked at the Server-based services strategy as a good idea, but not one that they want to see tied to a browser as the access mechanism. For every other vendor, the browser has been the leveler, the way for everyone to be able to access everything. But Microsoft has its Office application on over 500 million desktops so it was fairly certain that it could require an Office client as the access mechanism to additional server-based services and get the best of both worlds, a rich client and services from the web. As

Microsoft says, as technology evolves it never replaces what came before it; some things change; some things stay; some things are replaced

There will need to be more solutions in the long run and Microsoft will offer alternatives over time. A big issue is what happens as computing spreads to the emerging economies where the access device is unlikely to be the desktop computers so ubiquitous in the United States and much more likely to be phones, smartphones, or very small computers (we'll call them microcomputers). Many believe that such devices would be so small and inexpensive that Microsoft's operating system and office productivity suite would be too big and too expensive to be broadly implemented.

But Microsoft is likely to be working on software for just that eventuality. For example, it recently announced its Live Mesh network which synchronizes consumer devices and desktops. We suspect it will eventually synchronize all kinds of devices and also provide a cloud-based repository (or access to a repository) for document storage. Microsoft seems to have ambitious plans to enable software on many devices and computing from anywhere. We're not sure this is Live Mesh, but it is part of their ongoing strategy.

Microsoft views itself as a platform company with an ecosystem around it, and sees itself as building solutions on its own platform as well as having partners building solutions, too. Microsoft plans to continue to be a platform provider as they move into the cloud. After all, Microsoft claims, both partners and customers have the power of choice. They can make their own choices as to what goes into the cloud and what stays on the premises. This is likely to have a lot to do with governance, mission critical applications, and software that helps differentiate the company. Applications like email can go into the cloud; Microsoft can support both premises- and cloud-based email at the same time, so customers can pick and choose, move back and forth.

Microsoft expects that they will offer both everything as a service and everything on premise. Somewhere along that continuum will be the right spot for each customer. They will offer both browser and rich client access to the services in the cloud. (Note: I see a lot of future-talk here.)

Microsoft observes that we've been participating in the consumerization of technology: think cell phones, IM, Google. The IT pro isn't sure what his role should be. The right response is to let some things go to the cloud, leaving IT more time to work with business people and give them good solutions with more control, corporate solutions, with the IT pro becoming more of an adviser. The CIO has the responsibility to be sure that business data is controlled, governed, and so forth. We need to give him the tools and the resources to do this.

Microsoft sees the cloud as providing more technology as the base for partner-built solutions, allowing partners (and customers) to start building from a higher level.

Microsoft points to some of the SaaS activities they are participating in: Exchange and Dynamics CRM on line (through partners); services built on top of Microsoft services like Avalara which provides tax services for 12,500 U.S. tax jurisdictions; and Office across the cloud using hosted SharePoint and Exchange including very large customers like Energizer and CocaCola.

To summarize: Microsoft is moving to the cloud, both on its own and with partners. It sees itself as offering some of its services from the cloud as the basis for partners building services on top of them. In other cases, it sees its cloud-based services as a way to attract Office users and allow them to collaborate and access shared information. Time frames are not attached here so we suspect some of this might be at least a few years out.

Hosters provide infrastructure that anyone may employ. In the SaaS market, that would mean ISVs and various platform partners. Of course, hosters have been around for many years. Individual customers also use them to provide remote storage and computing, especially for applications that include frequent peaks and valleys in compute requirements or that include users in many locations. Hosters generally do not become involved in the implementation, management, or support of the applications running on their platforms.

Platform Partners also provide compute power and storage but they are likely (in the SaaS market) to also offer other inducements:

- They may have their own application that ISVs can build on top of (and use to attract customers), as Salesforce.com does.

- They may offer technical assistance in porting or rewriting existing applications to the SaaS environment, making it easier and faster for ISVs to prepare their applications for the SaaS market, as IBM and OpSource do.

- They may provide marketing resources to companies whose focus is mainly on creating great software rather than on getting it into customers' hands, as IBM, OpSource, and JamCracker do.

- They may offer the billing software that permits the ISV to readily offer his customers a variety of ways to flexibly pay for software, from free trials to monthly per seat payments to long-term, larger volume commitments. In many cases they can handle complex and sophisticated offerings, permitting ISVs to offer different combinations of modules and features to different users, billing the customer based only on actual usage or access, as Aria's platform partners do.

A platform player in the SaaS market is often labeled a Platform as a Service vendor or PaaS.

Triple Play

Intacct provides an on-demand accounting and financial management applications for SMB and enterprise businesses, as well as a connection to the Salesforce.com environment. It does that by partnering with Salesforce.com and IBM as well as its own ecosystem of partners. Think of it as a triple play.

Intacct automates key business processes from order entry through cash collection and procurement through vendor payment. The Intacct suite includes accounting, contract management, revenue recognition, inventory purchasing, vendor management, project management, financial reporting and business intelligence applications. Intacct integrates with other SaaS applications such as ADP, Paychex, Salesforce.com, OpenAir, and Adaptive Planning plus on premises and custom applications. Intacct is attracting a number of vendors who want to integrate with Intacct. Also, combining web services with Intacct permits solving real business problems. Vendors, not customers, have to make the products work together. This is very different than the traditional software model.

About 60% of Intacct's business is jointly delivered with Salesforce.com on IBM's SaaS infrastructure, an example of how SaaS can federate across multiple platforms and applications. Intacct is in charge of making its application integrate with other applications; they have their own ecosystem and do first level support while partnering for payroll, HR, etc., so customers can have best of breed solutions without having to deal with integration or compromise to avoid technical risk. Intacct's platform is the Internet, not Salesforce.com's APIs; they employ the Salesforce.com API to provide access to their data or application. APIs are hidden from customers and necessary changes are negotiated between Intacct and its partners. Users can employ wizards to builds their own automations or workflows on top of the applications to provide a mechanism for customer innovation.

Intacct uses multi-tenancy to be able to scale and enjoy other economic benefits of having many clients on a single infrastructure. They believe that while SaaS will not push all other types of software out of the market it will become a standard, the accepted way of building and deploying applications. That will drive R&D investments toward web-based applications, with more and more tools and applications being available there, rather than in more traditional environments and perhaps government regulations being rewritten to recognize the reality and the advantages of SaaS.

Intacct expects customers to make an annual or multi-year commitment, but payments may be made monthly, quarterly, or annually. An implementation fee to Intacct or an Intacct partner will also be charged. The products are marketed by Intacct and its ecosystem including Salesforce.com, IBM, resellers, and accounting firms. Their average sales cycle is five weeks.

Today, Intacct sees most of its competition in this $10 Billion market (its estimate) as coming from traditional software vendors. They target customers in companies with 25 to 500 customers. They believe vendors like NetSuite are still too small and too focused on the low end of the marketplace to be important to them and Workday is aiming for larger firms. Intacct is focusing for Life after QuickBooks; 60% of their customers are trading up and Intacct is the option instead of Lawson, Great Plains or Sage, where an average sale of

$150,000 in hardware, software, and services is much more expensive than Intacct's price point. The other 40% of their customers are changing from a mid-market product. Their ideal client is already using other SaaS products and is looking for a new accounting product so they can address the value of their accounting product without having to sell the idea of SaaS.

Billing is built into Intacct; usage information is captured in the back-end; IBM provides a hosting infrastructure for the Intacct platform.

For SaaS vendors, customer satisfaction is very important to keep those renewals and incremental revenues coming in. Their key question to customers is "Would you recommend us to your friend?" Currently, 90% of their customers say, "Yes."

SaaS vendors like Intacct are connecting in the cloud in an evolutionary way. Intacct started out with an API. Now, they're looking at moving up the stack and finding better ways to do things such as: single sign on; SLA; acceptable protocols; process support. Intacct tries to do a lot of industry advocacy around these issues because they feel they're out ahead of the industry, even ahead of where the very large SaaS vendors are, and it's their job to lead.

ISVs today come in three flavors:

Traditional Software Players offer software that is intended to be licensed by the customer for installation on his own hardware, within his own system. We often refer to such software as living "within the firewall," meaning it's within the customer's control. Most of the software before the era of the Internet fell into this category and even today most business software is still installed on customer hardware and managed by customer employees. It is that arrangement that SaaS may change, at least in part. Depending on your point of view, this is either an incredible opportunity to save money and redeploy scarce resources or a threat to the reliability and integrity of your data center.

Being Traditional and SaaS – Successfully

Open-Xchange is a provider of open source groupware that offers its solutions as both a Server Edition (which may be installed within company firewalls) and as a hosted version. In either case it facilitates teamwork and enables document sharing anywhere, anytime, with any device. Open-Xchange includes email integration, calendar, contacts, tasks, and document sharing with smart links between tasks and documents to facilitate teamwork and communication. Open-Xchange integrates with any email stack deployed, using APIs which permit tight integration. Should the implementation need an email application, they can bring in an open source solution.

Both the server and hosted versions are actively marketed and supported with over 3,500 companies on the server version (with more than 2 million server-based users) and millions of seats on the hosted version of Open-Xchange. They expect to have 7 million SaaS seats by the end of 2008, based on their current contracts and deployments. They achieve these huge numbers because their hosting partners are big players like Network Solutions (US), OVH (France), and Hostpoint (Switzerland).

Their strategy is to go after email replacement first, then groupware replacement with mobile support. Their next big opportunity is synchronization between mobile and desktop devices.

Their strategy is to start with a small average revenue per seat and then up sell in both their ISP and large end user accounts. Their goal is to multiply revenue ten times. They need to move users up the food chain to more sophisticated applications, because the market will become increasingly commoditized over time. Their goal is to create a partner ecosystem of ISVs so that where for example they are offering a virtual PBX, they can then offer address books, sophisticated calling capabilities, presence, and so forth.

To Open-Xchange cloud computing is all about reality meeting Web 2.0 and Mash-ups happening first on the desktop and the browser, but later with much more value for the end user at the server in the cloud.

Open-Xchange markets direct to its biggest accounts; it has a partnership with Parallels to reach smaller hosters and do integration with them. They are building an ISV channel for integration opportunities, and an ecosystem integration with Open-Xchange for both the SaaS and the traditional model. They might consider providing hosting for these ISVs with partners, especially for reaching vertical markets. They find that it takes two to six months to complete their sales cycle.

For competition, Open-Xchange looks to Microsoft Exchange, Google, and Yahoo. They view Notes and Groupwise as enterprise products and through their hoster partners they are going into much smaller companies that don't use these high-end products.

New versions of the hosted product are integrated on a regular basis. This dynamic shows up in many of the SaaS vendors we've interviewed.

On the other hand, a traditional (not quite software) vendor can decide to add a SaaS business to a very conventional paper-based business and find himself in a whole new world.

Iron Mountain's main business is storing boxes of paper for clients of every size. Its Digital Records Center for Images scans documents (receipts, financial statements, patient records, legal records, wills, anything) and stores them or sends them to clients via email or CD. They can store the image or perform OCR and store the digital information about the content. The paper can be stored or shredded. Shredding (and destruction of digital images) can be performed on a schedule to conform to federal regulations, industry usage, or organizational preferences.

This Digital Records Center is a new offering for Iron Mountain, started in 2007, and performed for a relatively small number of customers but is growing quickly.

The main advantage for an Iron Mountain client for this SaaS offering is speed. The system can be up and running in one to six weeks, compared to 12 to 18 months for a traditional content management system. Customers may scan the documents themselves or Iron Mountain partners can perform the scanning. There is a monthly fee for storage and usage (access).

Iron Mountain started out selling the product with a direct sales force in North America, selling to existing customers and new prospects. They are pleasantly surprised by the enthusiastic reception the offering is receiving. One afternoon of cold calls turned up 148 prospects who wanted to see a demo; a Webinar for 700 perspective customers led to 300 attendees who requested a follow up call. Iron Mountain finds that it takes two to twelve months in the sales cycle to close a deal.

Iron Mountain uses partners for scanning and partners with IBM for marketing and technology. Their main competitor is Xerox who offers similar services from a number of data centers, especially its Hot Spring, AK center.

The process lets customers create sophisticated combinations of stored files, including scanned paper files, pdf files, and wave files (such as an audio file from a deposition). Paper and digital storage can be combined. Paper records can be stored and only scanned when an image is required, rather than undergoing the expense to scan everything when only 1-2% of the total files are ever likely to be required. The digital files replace microfilm; they are easier to find than microfilm and since scanning them can be delayed until the image is required, substantial financial savings can be enjoyed for some applications.

New **Web-only** Players, sometimes referred to as **Net-Native**, are companies who came into existence to build software on the web, exploiting its capabilities. They can avoid the problems of the Traditional Software Players: they don't have to divide their corporate resources between two worlds, nor do they have to decide whether to address the entire market, or to try to protect their existing customer base.

On the other hand, these web-only start-ups get complete freedom as a trade-off for no customers; they frequently make compromises trying to get to critical customer mass quickly.

Typically, these new companies are attracted to economically attractive markets. That means they are looking for software markets that will attract large amounts of revenue, not the narrower vertical markets that many traditional software players happily operate in. This is partly because they are often venture financed (and venture capitalists are looking for a business model with a substantial payoff for the 10% or so of their investments that will be very successful). It is also because many of them go after horizontal rather than vertical applications that appeal to much larger markets.

Workday is the next act for an already successful software entrepreneur, David Duffield, the founder of People Soft, who left to start Workday after Oracle gobbled up his company and others in a giant acquisition play. This time, he had a plan right from the start and the discipline to know what the new company would focus on. Workday is designed to be a full-blown ERP company when it's finished, entirely net-native, focused on the high mid-market customer with 1,000 to 5,000 employees.

A plan this ambitious has to start somewhere and Workday's plan was to start with a Human Capital plan and then add modules in Financials and Procurement. That's what they've done. Their Human Capital Management product is in full production including payroll; Financial Management is in production; Resource Management (Procurement) is in production. Revenue (billing, service contract management) are futures.

For a young company selling to enterprises with a direct sales force, Workday is doing better than planned. They have 53 customers at my last contact; 25 sold and in production; 28 in the pipeline. They are finding that although their goal was high mid-market customers they are getting a smaller number of larger accounts and have already gotten several enterprise-size customers with as many as 20,000+ employees. Although they are doing the marketing themselves, against a typically three to six month marketing cycle, they are using partners for implementation, ranging from local specialists to Accenture-sized big, name-brand, systems integrators.

Customers pay an initial charge for implementation and then sign up for a three-to-five-year contract, calculated on a subscription basis.

From a competitive perspective, their market is higher-end than many SaaS vendors such as NetSuite. They are more likely to see SAP and Oracle. Some customers use Workday plus Taleo (a talent management software product), but Taleo wouldn't compete for the main human capital management functions.

Workday is now in its second complete year and it's moving up the curve in terms of size of customer; all their surprises are on the up side. Because they are seeing fewer deals at larger deal sizes, they are making more than they expected. (We suspect that they could eventually use partners to take them down into the mid-market where the direct sales force seems to be too busy to go.)

Business Partners might be platforms providers but they are more likely to be resellers, consultants, systems integrators, or others who assist the ISV in successfully marketing and implementing his SaaS application. In this, they are not very different than business partners of traditional software ISVs except that the services they are asked to provide may be briefer, the markets they can address may be at one and the same time larger (more customers) and smaller (in the size of the average customer), and the way compensation is made available from ISV partners will change, based on the way revenue flows in the SaaS market, so continuing annuities may be more commonplace than one-time fees.

Jamcracker is an aggregator who combines a variety of on-demand services so that they can be sold through various channels. Typically, they are another channel for the ISV, not the only channel (Note: A number of PaaSs and Aggregators will state this, but some platform providers, particularly those that provide assistance in getting traditional software vendors onto the SaaS platform, may be their sole route into the SaaS market.) Jamcracker believes that the challenge is for the companies in the second wave – new .Net companies, venture-funded, trying to get to the delivery stage – or established enterprise software companies trying to evolve a compliment to its existing license revenue to a new offering in the SaaS market to a market they previously didn't serve. Getting there can be difficult.

Some of Jamcracker's software partners include Cisco's

WebEx, McAfee, Microsoft (Exchange, Dynamics, and SharePoint), and IBM (Lotus, SameTime, Connect). They are frequently adding additional ISVs and recently added Zoho, itself a portfolio of desktop and collaborative applications. Their reseller partners range from large companies who sell under their own private labels, such as telcos, to small managed service providers, VARs, and consultants. Jamcracker does billing and low-level help for their application partners; the software is hosted at their data centers (or at partner data centers for some of their largest partners). They do systems management for some of their smaller ISVs. An integration tool kit allows service providers to publish and integrate their own software with the Jamcracker services they are providing to customers.

In this ecosystem, every solution partner is a potential reseller partner (of other solutions). It's a complicated system, but Jamcracker's role is tying together a lot of different services.

Jamcracker has almost four dozen ISV partners and over 100 reseller partners ranging from telcos to ISPs and VARS; this is three to four times as big as 12 months ago. Big partners can take a long time to acquire, as long as 18 months; small VARs might sign up in as little as a few days.

Jamcracker makes its money by taking a cut from every transaction. They have a master distribution agreement with ISVs and a wholesaler distribution agreement with resellers; they may have both with some companies, as companies reach for and fulfill their potential in this ecosystem.

Jamcracker sees itself as different than much of its competition in that it does not market to customer organizations, just to partners and ISVs. This is very different from the original Jamcracker model which was much more customer focused. They do look for customers with an existing customer base – this both guarantees that they will know what applications they are looking for and also that they have an immediate market to sell to.

Partners and Ecosystems

ISVs try to build an Ecosystem or supporting community of business partners around their application. This increases the value of the application to both potential buyers and to the ISV. It also makes each player in the ecosystem more valuable, since a larger set of partners attracts a larger number of customers, all potentially customers for each others' products and services.

Initially, ecosystems were built around applications. Now they may be built around platforms or around applications with their own APIs which function as platforms. In some of these more complex environments (Salesforce.com, discussed elsewhere, is a good example), it's sometimes hard to tell whether your partner is a platform or an application and perhaps it doesn't matter.

How is SaaS Different than Traditional SW?

SaaS is architecture for software development in which software is built as a set of services as well as a vehicle for software delivery. In this, it is something like SOA. Because of its design, SaaS can address issues such as operational efficiency, flexibility, simplicity, and guaranteed Service Levels (SLAs) that traditional ISVs are not expected to provide on their own.

SaaS	
Pros	*Cons*
No Capital Expenditure	Loss of Control
No or Minimal IT Resources	Possible Loss of Data
Faster Time to Use/ Value	Reliance on Service Provider
Lower Cost	Performance Issues
Flexibility	Hidden Set-Up Costs
Traditional Software	
Pros	*Cons*
Control	Requires Purchase of HW and SW
As much Reliability and Performance as IT wants to Buy	Requires Internal or Acquired Skills for Implementation and Management
Customization	Expensive to Upgrade
Built to User Requirements	Long Decision and Building Cycles
Integrated with Other IT Systems	

In a traditional software environment, the customer *buys* the software, as well as hardware to run it on and services to implement and manage it. To the extent that the customer wants the software to provide high levels of performance or reliability, he must take on this task himself, hiring staff with the appropriate skills, and buying additional hardware and software to provide what was called "system management" and what IBM has begun to call "services management." Alternatively, the customer can hire a system integrator to perform some or all of these tasks. Smaller customers may employ value-added resellers (VARs) who deploy their skills in particular geographies or vertical market segments.

Think of it as a trade-off line. Organizations can be more frugal and build systems that are less reliable or they can spend more money for more reliable systems with higher performance. Either decision can be right, depending on organizational needs. The best decision is likely to be a balance, somewhere in the middle.

It is possible to provide many of the same kinds of products using traditional and SaaS development, implementation, and distribution models, but some products – and some customer situations – are much better suited to SaaS. For that reason, nearly all new venture capital-supported new software development is for SaaS; investors think that's a better way to insure success in the marketplace.

On the other hand, we are likely to have many products in multiple versions around for a long time.

- Traditional software vendors who port or rewrite their software to SaaS are likely to continue to support their software (and customers) on their original platforms.

- Some SaaS vendors make the reverse migration. They start out offering a full net-native SaaS product but then discover that some customers (especially large enterprises with their own IT resources) prefer to run software within their own data center. Some SaaS vendors simply license the same software to the customer and support it; others provide a version that is optimized to a somewhat different environment or platform.

- There is a halfway-house, too. A SaaS vendor may discover that customers like the features of his product but are reluctant to run something outside their data center; on the other hand they're not large enterprises with self-sufficient IT staffs (or they are, but they're busy elsewhere or the application is very complex to implement and support). In that case, the application may be delivered as an appliance, loaded into its own server. Typically, the customer simply plugs it into his network, where it appears as a new service or application. Generally, the SaaS ISV will provide support for the application (unless the organization's IT department prefers to take on this task) and performs maintenance and upgrades to the software on the appliance remotely.

Some vendors offer all three versions: traditional, SaaS, and appliance, letting customers choose which one they prefer. Often, they make it easy for customers to use combinations of these technologies and to move from one to another as their needs change.

The SaaS model is inherently different than traditional software and that has implications for ISVs, service providers, and customers.

Chapter 2: Making the SaaS Decision

Deciding to Participate

It's hard *not* to hear about the SaaS market. New start-ups enter the market nearly every day, hoping that a brand new approach may be more compelling than a brand name. We'd observe that most new software companies today enter the market as SaaS companies or as hybrids (offering both SaaS and on-premises software). Existing (traditional) software vendors announce their entry to the SaaS market, too, sometimes hoping to expand into a new customer space, sometimes being pulled into SaaS by existing customers who prefer an on-line approach.

It's become difficult to find a venture capitalist that will make a software investment that is not in a SaaS-based company; they feel much of the future market is in this direction – and on-premises versions of SaaS products can be created later, if necessary. That gains the interest of any software company or potential start-up team. Getting to the decision to participate in the SaaS market can be a little more challenging.

The Opportunity

The software market is an over $200 billion global market growing at a 6% rate. Analysts project that 25-30% of new software will be bought from SaaS vendors by 2010, making it a huge market. That means that existing software companies will need to consider whether to move in the SaaS direction or risk being left behind.

It's not that SaaS will solve every problem for every business.

Many companies will continue to use their existing software solutions into the foreseeable future, especially for mission critical applications incorporating custom coding. But even these companies are looking at SaaS for some applications.

The opportunity varies, depending on where an ISV is coming from, from maintaining market position, to becoming the leader in a newly defined marketplace. One thing is certain; wait too long in a market which offers lots of economic opportunity and there are certain to be new SaaS players entering, cutting into the market share and brand recognition advantages of incumbent players.

Salesforce.com is one of the best known of the SaaS companies and is often used as an example of SaaS success. It is also an example of how a company uses market signals to change, over time, to meet market opportunities. Salesforce started out as a CRM application. Over time, it added an ecosystem of ISVs who sold their applications as part of a Salesforce environment. Salesforce recognized its opportunity and kept making it easier for partners to build applications on top of Salesforce until it became an industry platform and a software aggregator, offering many partner applications built to run on its platform.

Salesforce offers applications of its own for sales force automation, marketing automation, customer service and support, and partner relationship management. Its Platform as a Service, Force.com, lets a partner build and run any application without the need to create or deploy infrastructure, leading to faster time to value for both partners and their customers, and providing integration across a variety of applications from many sources. AppExchange, Salesforce's application marketplace, delivers web-based applications on demand from Salesforce's many partners. A new Checkout application will allow customers to buy programs directly on-line. Salesforce will provide first level support for these programs, passing 2nd level support back to the ISV. AppExchange applications are guaranteed to work together; they are all native to the Salesforce platform, although some have non-native parts that were not written in APEX or Visual Force. AppExchange can include these native and composite applications plus integrated applications which are integrated into Salesforce but hosted separately (Intacct, mentioned elsewhere, is a good example).

Salesforce sees this new mechanism for easily acquiring applications particularly appealing in the SMB market (up to 1,000 employees) where the organization has a small IT staff and doesn't want to bother with integration. They believe that most enterprise (large) customers will want direct engagements; they may use AppExchange, but Salesforce is not sure to what extent, since enterprises have both ongoing relationships with systems integrators and in-house resources. Of course, immediacy is a drive for both SMBs and departments in large companies and we suspect it's what will make the AppExchange applications appealing. There are 350 partners on AppExchange and most will sell their applications directly through the Checkout store.

Many of the applications are written by ISVs who are also systems integrators. They will develop and implement the applications on the Salesforce platform but they will package the intellectual property and use it for their own customer(s) as well as sell it more generally.

Salesforce is a public company with $1 billion in revenue and about 47,000 customers.

They divide their sales force into two teams.

a) The SMB General Business Group is highly transactional. It uses an inside sales team. Salesforce does the implementations for these customers. The telemarketing people are like order takers and can close the deals, against a typical one to three month sales cycle. Sales are turned around very quickly against one to three year contracts. No one does month to month.

An SMB might be charged an implementation fee, really a conversion fee, if they want Salesforce to do services work or integration for them. They could choose to do it themselves or hire their own consultant. Salesforce is hiring some architects to guide third party service providers in the implementation process.

b) The Enterprise group typically rolls out whole divisions. They may buy all the seats for the year and have a two to three year contract. Sometimes they have an agreement to ramp up users year by year but lock in pricing.

Salesforce directly markets to enterprises. Mid-market firms sometimes move to this direct marketing and sometimes use service companies for design and implementation help. Enterprise firms may look at competition and consider their business needs; they are typically looking at a pain point and considering solutions. Salesforce has high close rates, but in the Enterprise, with an average close of three months, actual closes can run as high as 18 months, depending on when they are looking to implement the product.

Salesforce agrees that Microsoft is a competitor in the SMB space and also NetSuite. They also see SalesLogix, SugarCRM, Siebel, PeopleSoft, SAP moving to a SaaS system, Oracle with Siebel, Oracle on Demand, and so forth. But they show well against these firms and their partner portfolio helps as does their market position.

Textics demonstrates how a very technical application can, with appropriate interfaces, become a useful service in the web environment. When I first heard about Textics Talklets server-based text-to-speech system, instantly converting text on an HTML web page into clear sound files audible to a web visitor, I was bemused. It sounded too technical for its environment. But 100 companies with about 1 million users are using Talklets, so the proof is in the using.

The application requires connectivity between the active browser window and the Talklets speech servers. Converted text is delivered back to end users as optimized and streamed MP3 files, delivered from a unique combination of newly processed and cached audio elements. Rules can be applied generically or tuned on a site-by-site basis and specific languages or voices can be associated with particular user accounts. Supplementary keyboard control and right click spoken thesaurus and dictionary are standard.

Later in 2008, Textic will launch a proxy browser system, Talklets Anywhere that will allow users to vocalize any website.

Talklets can be added to any website with simple Javascript and can be customized in function and look to meet site design guidelines. Talklets can employ a toolbar floating in the browser and a toolbox embedded within the page layout (which can be controlled by individual buttons or icons, as the site style might require). Both the toolbar and the toolbox can be branded with a company logo or style.

Textic was conceived and developed as a SaaS only application. It is marketed to extend the use of text-to-speech from being primarily an accessibility enhancement (to meet requirements for serving the disabled market) to a mainstream website function to increase the duration and stickiness of visits.

The product is sold directly via on-line sales to small and medium enterprises and through relationship-based sales to larger enterprises. There is also a program to develop strategic relationships with relevant major corporations. Low value sales may be immediate self-service events; long-term private label relationships with major companies take a long time to develop.

The Competition

There is lots of competition. Most traditional software vendors are looking at the SaaS market or already participating in it. Of course, some of them will wait to move until it's too late – or they'll do a bad job of understanding the elements of becoming a successful SaaS vendor. Since we can't guess which ones will do that, it's well to assume that traditional software vendors will be competitors in the SaaS market, too.

Many analysts believe the real competition will be the new companies who can implement web hosted solutions which fully exploit Internet technology without the need to be burdened by their previous technology or marketing decisions. They're thinking of Google vs. Microsoft. But remember that most new companies are small and under-funded and most existing companies are running successful businesses, with good customer relationships. With some guidance, traditional software companies should be able to compete, even if their solutions are a little different than those of the start-ups, with more emphasis on backward compatibility and interoperability with legacy investments.

The scenarios we've presented in this book are a mix of traditional software vendors moving to the web and new start-ups to give you an idea of how it's working. The next set of scenarios is a good example. Microsoft Project is the best known project management software and that has made it a high profile goal for many SaaS start-ups, looking for a product category. We've selected two.

We wanted to present two points of view on project management software because it's a category which is so well suited to the SaaS environment. Traditional project management software is a heavyweight application, hard to learn and hard to use. Generally, a few people use it on behalf of the organization and it's rarely up-to-date since information must funnel through that bottleneck. In the SaaS world a new developer can create a new version of project management, simplified and designed for everyone to access as much of the application as they might need. This has attracted a number of players.

Needless to say, they approach the problem from different points of view. Some software emphasizes planning; others may be more about project execution, process management and control. An emphasis on collaboration may be built right in, so that the project management users do not need to go elsewhere to discuss the project. This can be especially compelling when the project includes participants across many locations and from separate organizations who may not have other convenient collaboration tools.

Clarizen is a provider of on-demand, collaborative project execution software; the emphasis is on supporting the team doing the execution across their different locations and organizations. Globalization has created a business opportunity for SaaS-based project management, since there are now more issues to manage and management is pressured to proceed at a faster pace. Project Management lets companies manage more professionally, sensing and responding to the issues they face.

Clarizen markets their product over the web and via telesales, responding to leads from their site and Google-based free trials. Approximately 5% of their free trials convert to paid customers in a tidy three week sales cycle. Their major growth problem is generating enough leads. They encourage customers to sign a one-year contract with a 50% discount, but allow customers to buy month-to-month with a $50 per seat per month charge. There are no up-front fees and customers are offered one-hour free webinar training. Additional training is available by webinar at a fee.

Most of Clarizen's customers are small to mid-sized companies (in the 100 to 3,000 employee range), especially service companies managing multiple locations. Clarizen's focus is on customer acquisition and establishing their brand, their value proposition, and their ability to respond to customer problems with good solutions. Over time, as they want to sell more seats and additional products into a growing customer base, they will have to focus more on customer service and satisfaction.

Projity is designed to be a complete, on-demand replacement of Microsoft Project. It also has a version, Project-on-Demand, which is integrated with Salesforce.com, so Projity activities and milestones populate within Salesforce.com task lists and calendars, showing as completed within both applications and updated in the project schedule. It may be used as a new product or as a Microsoft Project replacement, opening existing Project files.

Fewer than half of Projity's 200 customers are on the Salesforce platform; the rest run on Projity's own data center. Projity itself is application-centric; they are not a platform. Their multi-tenant design allows them to be as efficient as possible, with users self-administering their own sign-up and usage and automated provisioning, avoiding time and complexity barriers for the users.

They are now offering OpenProj, an open source desktop which is a free download (there have been 600,000 downloads), hoping to convert organizations to a paid subscription product, but they believe that many customers will choose to have some users on the free Open Source Desktop (which Projity will agree to support) and others on a paid subscription. Projity also supports the idea that users may pay for Projity only when they need it, activating the product in months when they are working on a project, and de-activating it (and not paying for it) in months when users are working on other tasks.

This is a much lighter-weight product, not so much in sense of function, but in the sense that it's less of a burden to users and less of a financial cost to organizations. That could lead to more use of project management.

The Dynamic and evolving nature of the SaaS Marketplace

Like everything in the technology marketplace, the SaaS marketplace doesn't stand still; everything is changing all the time. This means planning an entry into the SaaS market requires planning to hit a moving target. It also means planning for the market as it will be when you enter it – not the market as it exists on the day you decide you'd like to be a SaaS player. There could be additional players, changes in platforms, features, or pricing. A company that wants to be a successful ISV keeps all of that in mind.

The Price of Not Participating

No ISV has to offer a SaaS solution. A new ISV could offer a traditional solution and he might find customers. In fact, for certain kinds of applications, customers still favor traditional on-premises solutions. But such a developer would have to be prepared to fund the project himself and fight hard to get noticed in a market where everyone is looking for new SaaS products.

An existing traditional software vendor can just sit there continuing to service his existing customers and hoping that SaaS is a fad that is going to go away. But the odds are against that. More than 70% of IT customers surveyed in 2006 noted that they were either already using SaaS or they were planning to use it within 12 months. Vendors, who think SaaS is just for the SMB market, may be surprised and enlightened by looking at the customer lists of SaaS vendors. Many easily recognized big businesses appear. It's not that enterprises are giving up their IT departments, but rather that they are augmenting their IT resources with another computing alternative. We would expect this trend to continue and for firms of every size to use some SaaS software. Of course, for the SMB market, SaaS offers a new opportunity to use first class applications without the cost of a full-blown IT department or the time to implement complex software – three to four times as long as it takes to bring up a comparable SaaS application. Already, a few SMB firms are running entirely in the SaaS environment; we may see more of this in the future.

Making Good Decisions to Assure SaaS Success

It's important to go into SaaS with eyes wide open – there's a lot to see. An existing ISV needs to understand all of the financial implications of the SaaS model on his existing business, whether he intends to launch a new business to complement an existing traditional software model or whether the ultimate goal is to be "all SaaS."

None of this can happen unless ISV management is firmly on board. This means they want to be in the SaaS business. You'd like them to be enthusiastic about the opportunity but reasonable in their expectations about what the costs and revenues will look like, especially when you're getting started. It helps a lot if others in your market sector are already successfully offering SaaS; then the competitive spirit will help them make the commitment.

Moving to SaaS isn't free. It may require a substantial investment in software development. Some ISVs simply move their existing software to a hosted platform. Others completely rewrite their application, incorporating improvements and changes to exploit the web/hosted environment. You'll need to consider this decision carefully. If your application appeals to very large numbers of users, it's likely that an application written from scratch for the web will ultimately appear (if it hasn't already); you may need to plan to do that, too, in order to compete. But if you offer a business application in a vertical segment, with few competitors, and a specialized customer set where your knowledge of the market is as valuable as the code in the application, a good port to the hosted platform may be all you need.

Net-native Start-ups need to do a readiness check, too. They have to be certain they have enough capital (or a plan to get some) for the development, deployment, and initial marketing period. Knowing that even very large software companies don't make their deadlines, there needs to be sufficient buffer time and money for reasonable contingencies. If you're going to market through partners, you need to allow for time after there is something compelling to show, to recruit the partners and get initial sales and marketing materials ready.

As you're deciding what to do and when to do it, looking at what the successful SaaS players are doing can be an excellent example. In many cases successful players and partners will be glad to provide guidance and help. After all, more successful SaaS players help the market to grow. Your application may be less a competitor and more a helpful addition to someone's ecosystem.

Chapter 3: Planning for Success in SaaS

The New Business Model

It's harder to change from being a traditional software vendor to being a SaaS vendor (or a hybrid) than to simply start as a SaaS vendor. That's because you have to change so many things that are working and companies find it hard to change. Some of what follows will be more useful to traditional vendors contemplating making the change to SaaS; other parts will be useful to both existing ISVs and new SaaS start-ups.

Planning the New Financial Model

Because SaaS has become the Next New Thing, many ISVs (new and old) rush into it with little or no understanding of how their company will make revenue and profits. Of course, on some level they hope that revenue will be quickly coming in as a steady stream, rather than in big lumps, but they have great difficulty understanding the implications of this kind of cash flow. They also have had little insight into what their expenses might be and how long it might take to reach a breakeven point, much less profitability. This requires:

- Advance planning so that the ISV organization understands the up-front expenses they will be required to pay. This will vary, of course, depending on the application, the ambitions of the company, and whether it is an existing organization or a start-up, but all of these expenses are nevertheless likely to occur. They might include software development and/or porting, recruiting a new sales force and channel partners, marketing, paying for the supporting infrastructure (capital expense and labor to build and run it or rental fees to use an existing data center) and implementation, management, and ongoing support for the application.

Just how this works varies from ISV to ISV, of course.

a) Traditional ISVs will presumably have an existing business and cash flow which might provide some staff and infrastructure to get started and some cash.

b) Start-ups have no existing customers to service and they are more likely (if they have an appealing application and an intelligent approach) to be able to eventually qualify for venture investment; this could provide not only some capital, but also advice to get them past some of the known problems. Of course, it also means that they are giving up large amounts of ownership and control.

- All of this is occurring in a marketplace that is changing every day. New products are announced, new firms enter, and new ideas about how to solve technological problems appear and are dismissed, or become ubiquitous solutions (remember life before the Internet? Before wireless? Before virtualization?). For example:

  o Many users are moving to employing web-based services instead of software applications. The users don't think of themselves as using a piece of software running on a complex infrastructure (which, thanks to a well-designed user experience they never see).

  o All the owners of information can, under these circumstances, become service providers, competing for user attention, and adding additional services (software) that they are probably acquiring in the marketplace. The provider could be the user's IT department, an ISV, or a SaaS provider or other Service Provider.

- o In that world (where the user thinks he is getting a service rather than the use of software), payment gets very fuzzy, and is likely to be "free" (perhaps internal IT costs) or advertising supported.

Sales and Marketing

Marketing Costs

Many Net-native SaaS ISVs think that just putting their software on the web is marketing. It isn't. Most go beyond that and the most popular plan is to offer free trials for individuals or small groups in the hope that they will then go back and sell their organization on the paid version of the software. It works. There are also attempts to sell a more fully-featured version of the SaaS product (or a supported version) as an upgrade, even to individual users. That is generally less successful.

None of these are really free since there is acquisition costs associated with letting prospective buyers know that something interesting is going on and getting them to come download the free software or whatever they need to access your SaaS application. Once they're signed up, they need to be marketed to on an ongoing basis to upgrade their participation and/or go talk to their company. Web advertising will work for the initial acquisition; electronic mail, newsletters, and telemarketing work for the upgrade campaigns.

ISVs may also outsource customer acquisition, using third-party marketing firms to do telemarketing and building a business partner ecosystem to sell their SaaS product. Many SaaS providers partner with established market players like

IBM and leverage the awareness, demand generation, and branding support these seasoned partners can provide.

Customer retention is harder, based on some combination of pricing and satisfaction that is perceived value. To be successful in the SaaS business requires a high customer retention rate so you can focus much of your marketing attention on adding new customers, not replacing departing ones. This means constant attention to the marketplace to be certain your product is competitive in both features and pricing and, more important, constant attention to customer satisfaction with service.

Especially with monthly contract SaaS offerings, customers are only a click or two away from selecting another vendor if they feel they're not getting enough service, enough performance, or enough attention. A SaaS vendor's job is to make sure that doesn't happen.

You want to anticipate dissatisfaction and let the customer know you're unhappy that they might have occasion to be unhappy – like the Starbucks I had coffee at last week. I had a very long wait for my coffee after it was ordered – maybe 5 of 6 minutes – and when it was delivered, it came with an apology for the wait and a card good for a free coffee next time, guaranteeing that I'd be back. That's attention to customer retention.

Of course, if your customers have to spend two months getting set up and pay $150,000 for the privilege (to say nothing of signing a three year contract), they're less likely to leave at the first whiff of dissatisfaction, but it's still your job to keep them happy.

Adding Value as a SaaS ISV

It's not just enough to be a SaaS ISV; it's important to add value in a way that would otherwise not be available.

In this chart we list some of the kinds of customers SaaS vendors target and some of the kinds of added value they may offer to each category. Function and features are, of course, required; it is the services, flexibility, and other services SaaS can bring that prove its value.

Category	Added Value
Offering SaaS to End User Customers	• Function • Features
SaaS Offering as a Stand-Alone Profit Center	• Function • Features • Support • Services
SaaS Offering as a Compliment to on-Premise Offering	• Function, Features • Support, Service • Flexibility
SaaS Offering as a Trial of Enterprise on-Premise Offering	• Reaching a new audience
Arms Supplier Offering	• Adding thousands (or millions) of customers
Solutions that Include 3rd Party SaaS (Integrator)	• Integrated solution • Incremental solution (80% already done)

Some ISVs start out selling their own tools and applications and then go on to integrating partners' applications into a broad portfolio offering. Eventually, this can let them move into another business as a supplier (arms dealer) to larger aggregators.

Etelos started out writing tools to support its own business, selling phone systems. They wrote their own CRM system and a newsletter system to support their business. The newsletter business grew to a service until the Internet bubble burst when Etelos went to developing and distributing web-based applications and building custom applications and tools.

In late 2006, Etelos partnered with Google to build CRM and Project Management products for Google Apps. They have moved to a platform which provides these applications within an environment where small businesses can select on-line applications to license and deploy within the hosting environment of their choice as well as to employ them seamlessly together. Developers can use the platform to develop, license, sell, and support their applications. The Etelos CRM and project management applications drive developer products and customer awareness to the marketplace as the developer partners build the applications which they will monetize on the platform.

We asked CEO Jeff Garon how Etelos (which is publicly traded on the OTC market) is different than Salesforce.com. He replied that, of course, they're competitive; in being a platform with a CRM application and developer partners, but Etelos offers a broader portfolio with a few technical advantages, like being able to provision multiple applications simultaneously. In any case, Garon said, "It's such a big environment we need other marketplaces to be successful to drive our success." That's classic. Young new vendors have to rely on established players to define and educate markets.

Etelos is considering white-labeling its portfolio for large partners but it isn't prepared to talk specifics yet. Its focus is clearly on the SMB market and it expects to remain there while some competitors, like Salesforce.com find it appealing to move up market to enterprise customers. Some Etelos partners are looking for a small number of seats; some sell quite a few; it's the combination that counts. Partners are looking for $1-1.5 million in revenue for their site, but they have to keep remembering they are looking for SMB business not the enterprise. Etelos' goal is hundreds of partners.

Etelos currently has 21 partners with 39 applications, including vertical applications. They have about 10,000 customers on their own applications and over 5,000 accounts. The marketplace was only launched in June, 2008 so it's a bit early to talk about partners' customers.

Etelos will make its money by revenue sharing with partners, advertising, providing professional services and hosting to its partners, and doing white labeling. A partner who takes more of their services (consulting, hosting) might pay a lower revenue share. For many of their partners they are an incremental channel of distribution, so partners are willing to see what they might obtain in a more flexible spirit.

Etelos markets through search engine advertising, viral marketing, and speaking and exhibiting at conferences. They collect leads and follow them up via direct mail and a dedicated in-house sales force. The Etelos Marketplace platform connects developers, customers and solutions, providing them with viable alternatives to the usual enterprise software applications sold by major vendors with direct sales forces.

A Completely Different Distribution Model Needs a Different Sales Plan

SaaS may be software, but selling it requires rethinking the conventional software sales plan.

In the past, ISVs hired software salesmen who could follow up expensively acquired customer leads (gained through trade shows, advertising, seminars, and references) and persevere in following them through a lengthy sales cycle. Six to twelve months was not unusual and 18 months was not unheard of.

As a reward, salesmen received hefty percentages of the software's sales price at the time the deal was consummated, made possible because customers typically paid for software up-front, and then paid annual maintenance fees of 15- to 20%. Good software salesmen could make hundreds of thousands of dollars a year.

Obviously, you won't be selling most SaaS offerings with a team of suited salesmen with briefcases. There are some big deals to close in the SaaS market – think of selling a SaaS offering to a customer with 10,000 or more desktops – but they are the exception. (SaaS vendors selling enterprise software to enterprise customers do use a high-end direct sales force.) Since you can't offer the kind of compensation plan a typical "big time" software salesman would expect, you shouldn't plan to use typical software salesmen.

Instead it is common to use a combination of marketing (web ads, for example) and indirect sales (telemarketing, business partner sales). These will need new compensation methods, because much of the revenue from the sale is coming later. ISVs with deep pockets may be able to pay compensation up front and then enjoy the monthly payments. More likely, they'll share continuing revenue payments with sales partners.

In the SaaS business, money changes hands differently. In many cases, customers can use small amounts of the software for free as a limited time trial or even permanently. This is to prevent the cost of the software from being a barrier to showing and selling it when, for all intents and purposes, it costs the vendor almost nothing for a single user to employ it. Once an organization decides to buy a SaaS product, they have many ways of purchasing it:

1. Most products are priced by the "seat" (user) per month. This dates back to the early days of the market when it was literally possible to go to an ASP site and buy the

software for 30 days at a time with a credit card. Most software cost less than $50 per user per month so this was a reasonable idea. If the user decided he didn't like the software, he simply cancelled his account. If he decided it was just what his company needed, he could sign up for more seats.

2. But most SaaS software today isn't sold by the month. SaaS companies want a one to three year commitment from user organizations and for many applications the set up costs are substantial enough that the idea of clicking from one vendor to another is no longer realistic. However, even if a three-year contract is signed, the customer may be paying on a monthly, quarterly, or annual basis. There will be a one-time set-up or services charge, which varies, depending on the product and on the data bases and legacy applications the user organization needs to attach to. It can be substantial, but it's nothing like the design and implementation costs of a major traditional software project. Think at least an order of magnitude less; maybe two orders.

3. Most of this revenue can't be recognized by the SaaS vendor up front, since the service will be delivered over time. It's like selling subscriptions to magazines. The service sits on your book as a liability and you need to be sure you can fulfill it or return the money you received.

4. That means salesmen can't be paid huge commissions up front either. In the beginning this wasn't a problem, since most ASP/SaaS vendors didn't think they needed salesmen to sell their products. They assumed it was a "field of dreams" moment: if you build it they will come. Unfortunately, it doesn't work that way. *Consumer* SaaS software like Google Docs is largely a viral marketing, word of mouth, PR on the web, phenomenon. Business software is not.

So SaaS software is sold be a combination of web-based advertising, specialized blogs and newsletters, webinars, some face-to-face events, especially trade shows and seminars, telemarketing (especially for following up leads), and actual software salesmen for marketing to enterprises, especially for software that is intended for the IT department or that will impact the entire organization. These salesmen are not unlike the software salesmen of old (and frequently come from sales organizations like Oracle and IBM), but SaaS companies have to either have deep pockets to pay them in the traditional up-front, at the time of sale way, or new methods that split compensation between some up-front rewards and some deferred compensation that over time will create an annuity stream for the successful salesman.

It can be hard to ease your way into the SaaS market when so many new expenses have to be paid up front before any new revenues occur. OpSource is a platform provider for SaaS who prices its platform to help SaaS start-ups avoid large front-end costs and spread them over their revenue stream.

OpSource is a platform vendor, providing web operations for "serious" SaaS and web businesses. (This is their way of saying that they're in the business-to-business sector, rather than consumer software.) OpSource's On-Demand service combines technical, applications, and business operations together so that the ISV does not need to worry about investing in a data center or maintaining the staff to implement and manage his application delivery. They provide everything but the application itself. Their customers are charged only on the basis of what they sell, not on the basis of the resources they consume. This is very appealing to start-ups.

OpSource also provides a complete Billing application, either integrated with its On-Demand service, or as a stand-alone application. Its Connect service allows customers to publish multiple services across a common, secure platform and can unify SaaS applications in the cloud with legacy applications behind the firewall.

OpSource describes their customers as one-third traditional software companies making a move to SaaS – companies like BMC, Business Objects, and Adobe. Two-thirds of its customers are dedicated SaaS companies, mainly start-ups.

Customers usually come to OpSource when they are launching their application. However, in the last six to twelve months, they are starting to get companies who are already up and running on their own infrastructure moving over to OpSource. Taleo (a human capital management company) would be a good example. Perhaps the SaaS application is less than 100% of their business. Perhaps they initially built the infrastructure themselves because they thought that would be cheaper but then discover that it's a lot of work and hard to scale as they grow. OpSource can offer them better compliance, better tools and analytics, and typically they're cheaper – as little as 10-15% of what they're spending.

OpSource has 200 customers representing millions of users on their infrastructure and over a billion transactions per day. They are hosting about 250 applications of which 75 to 80% are multi-tenant.

OpSource's differentiation is its business model. It charges customers based on what their revenue stream is doing rather than on what they bought for infrastructure. There is a set-up fee and then customers pay by transaction or by user or by a percentage of revenue (their billing software supports any variation), depending on the customer and the application. Their cost for technical operations depends on the amount of usage; traditional SaaS platform vendors price at server capacity; OpSource doesn't – the customers can have options. It's really using another way of calculating usage but the customer CEO's and product managers love it. Their operations guys always want to look at server usage. OpSource's average contract length is two years, but more business can always get a better price.

OpSource's Treb Ryan is outspoken in his opinion about multi-tenancy. He believes that the real difference is cost and that the leverage goes in opposite directions. Multi-tenant gets better and better, Treb says, while multiple instances of single tenant gets worse and worse after its limit. He thinks that the next generation of SaaS, integration in the cloud, will require multi-tenancy for price efficiency because it has such a big impact on the ISVs financials, but also because updating the application becomes difficult over time for non-multi-tenant applications. He looks at multi-instance as an interim measure. (We'd point out that for some ISVs, facing little or no competition, the interim could be a long time.)

OpSource does mainly web-based marketing, using traditional conferences for lead generation. It does successful webinars based on customer case studies – they just can't be advertisements. They also run the SaaS Summit, an industry forum, and have established themselves as experts.

They find that thinking about a sales cycle for OpSource is a bit more complex than just picking a number. They'd estimate 60 to 90 days from first discussion to sale, but that doesn't account for ISVs they talk to who then disappear for two years and show up to close the sale within 90 days of their next cycle of discussions – they just weren't ready the first time. Microsoft, Salesforce, and some of their ecosystem partners all help with lead generation.

OpSource has lots of competitors, depending on which category you're considering. So Aria in billing; Informatica in Connect; Rackspace and Amazon in technical.

They view themselves as being in a good position for cloud computing with their expertise and experience and their client portfolio – perhaps as middleware for the cloud.

Product Design

There are many routes to SaaS. An existing ISV can take a traditional software application, make a few small changes, and get it onto a fairly basic SaaS platform in a relatively short time (weeks or a few months). In this form, it will usually require its own server and each instance of the application will require a copy of the software. With virtualization software, it may be possible to get around this requirement.

However, this rough-and-ready approach to getting an existing application to the SaaS environment is unlikely to take advantage of the features of the web.

A Different Design Model can Lead to Different Products

Each ISV gets to decide where to make his investments. It is the selection process that is difficult.

Existing ISVs must decide whether to take their existing software products to the SaaS market, building identical or similar SaaS versions, or whether to build entirely new SaaS products. These products might be newly thought out products for their existing customers and market, exploiting web features and technology, and incorporating the ISVs expertise, or they might be entirely new products, aimed at new applications or even (riskier) new customers. Usually ISVs mitigate risk by either building new products for existing customers or extending existing products to new customers. That allows them to leverage their brand and reputation in introducing their new offering.

The SaaS model is designed to let users take on more of some responsibilities and less of others.

1. SaaS products should be self-administering; that means users should be able to sign up new users and new projects themselves (within policies set by their organizations), rather than sending requests through an administrative chain of command that is slow and costly for the organization and frustrating for the users.

2. Users should be able to make small configuration changes (making selections from menus) that make the applications suit them better, without programming.

3. Users should not have to worry about how the software gets installed, whether it is compatible with the hardware or with other, pre-existing software, or how it is integrated with other, relevant data in their environment. This should occur automatically as part of the SaaS product's set-up process and on-going management.

The SaaS model combines what the software offers to the users (features/functions) and how the software is delivered. Both parts are equally important. If the features and functions are not compelling to the target audience, the software is not likely to succeed in its market (although giving away less functional software for free, especially to a less demanding audience, can in itself create a market, as Google has discovered). If the distribution model is not efficient it will be hard for the ISV or his distribution partners to satisfy their customers and make money. Many service providers argue that SaaS products must be multi-tenant (able to run multiple sessions on a single server simultaneously) in order to provide efficient use of infrastructure and provide satisfactory performance.

Because the balance between features, usability, and programmability and customization change between traditional software and SaaS, it is designed to appeal more to users and (perhaps) less to traditional IT departments. In the long run, they will come to understand that many applications can be better provided to users via SaaS, conserving their skills for applications which require new architectures, complex integration, and custom programming to support business goals. But in the short run, there is bound to be some initial hostility.

Zoho offers a suite of on-line collaborative productivity and business applications for knowledge workers. They have 16 applications plus the new Zoho Docs (a repository for document sharing), recently announced.

Zoho is part of AdventNet, a larger originally traditional software company with interests (besides Zoho) in network and systems management, security, database search and migration, and test automation tools. The Zoho division itself has 250 developers working on Zoho.

Zoho has about 40% of its users in the consumer and student category; the rest are business users. Zoho had about one million users at the end of the second quarter of 2008 and adds about 100,000 users every four to five weeks. They are hoping to add at least one million users in the next year.

Zoho is trying to following AdventNet's business model. That is, assemble a large portfolio of related products. Different customers will start with different initial products and then expand to others on the portfolio. The idea is to offer all the tools a business needs to run their business on-line. (Note: At this moment in time, this probably means a focus on smaller businesses.)

Zoho's business model is both easy and complicated. For individuals, all the products are free. Business products are packaged together with additional services and charged (after the first 10 users) at $50 per seat per year. Business products are charged by the product, but each product is priced differently. For example, the CRM product is free for the first three users and $12 per user per month after that; project management is based on the number of projects and users; invoices are based on the number of invoices. The system keeps track of everything and sends a single bill every month.

Zoho markets through trade shows, web marketing and customer referrals. They don't gather leads and follow them up. They count on their free usage model to bring in customers. They do a lot of their marketing through partners; they have 100 worldwide partners and 2,400 resellers in China alone. It's the partners that do the marketing and build up the user base. Many partners are telcos or private label service providers. Their target market is companies with up to 30 employees (Zoho comes from SoHo), maybe less than 50, certainly less than 100. Although that being said, they have a customer who uses their CRM application for 250 users and AdventNet uses Zoho for their 950 employees.

They get an occasional request to deploy Zoho inside the firewall and have some pilots in process. The idea would be an appliance where the software would run inside the firewall but Zoho would do the updating and upgrading. They might offer some coordination for the customer on updating.

Zoho doesn't see themselves as having a competitor, although, of course, Google competes with some of their applications on the consumer side. They feel that no vendor offers the breadth of their portfolio so they compete with many vendors, while a customer could need only one vendor if they selected Zoho.

Chapter 4. The Economic Life Cycle of Software Applications

In deciding which products to move to the SaaS platform, ISVs should consider the economic life of the products he's thinking of moving or building.

An ideal product is one which has a large enough market to guarantee plenty of customers – more than any one ISV could possibly require – but not so many as to attract large players with unlimited budgets to build or acquire software. An existing traditional software ISV, particularly one in a vertical market, may already be in this situation, servicing a comfortable number of customers, but not so many as to attract too much competition. One that has no competition at all might safely choose to wait for customers to ask for SaaS-based applications, but he should know that he might be giving up a chance to market to unidentified customers whom SaaS vendors in closely-related markets might find a way to service. In that case, by the time he enters the SaaS market, he may find that in spite of his strong position in the traditional software market in his segment, he will find it difficult to establish a strong position in the SaaS market.

Mainstream products which appeal to the broad market – accounting, CRM. ERP, supply chain, human resources management, collaboration – are very large markets. All of them have already attracted strong SaaS players and even strong traditional software suppliers are finding it difficult to now enter this market with SaaS offerings. An excellent example would be Siebel which did not take Salesforce seriously and waited too long to come into the SaaS market –

and then with a product which was not viewed as strongly as their traditional offering. A traditional software vendor in one of these markets who isn't developing a SaaS offering may already be too late unless he has an exceptional idea in mind. A new net native ISV would need to have a great idea, strong financial backing, and superior execution to have a chance in these very competitive spaces. Workday who we've mentioned earlier, would be a good example.

Of course, the economics are not everything. ISVs of any type should look for SaaS products which can exploit the web as a delivery platform and which can exploit web features as part of the software. A SaaS product which can both exploit the web and which has strong economics should be a potential winner.

Sometimes, ISVs are not looking for products to port or new SaaS products to build, but rather for SaaS products to acquire and distribute. Service Providers (SPs) also look for SaaS products which can use distribution partners to find their markets. These companies will be looking for products that are far enough along to be at least at the prototype or pilot stage. Often, they would rather look at products that have revenue or customers (although they rarely wait for products with profits, since they can make the best deals before start-ups reach that point). They look for SaaS companies that have:

- Well-defined products which are ready or nearly ready for the marketplace.

- Products that exploit the SaaS model.

- Products that are either associated with widely accepted standards or are built to the prospective partner's own APIs.

- Products which fit into the acquiring vendor's portfolio

(and will appeal to his customer set, lowering marketing costs).

Is Customization Supportable? How much and How?

In the ASP round, customization and products designed to be used on-line, shared by many customers, were thought to be mutually exclusive. ISVs who customized their product in order to sign on one more customer ended up with multiple versions of their product to support and became hosters rather than ASPs, losing any economic advantage.

As we moved to the SaaS round, many ISVs redesigned their products. The goal was to provide some customization without interfering with the SaaS business model, which many thought required offering all customers the same product to permit economies of scale.

This led to products that could have limited amounts of customization. ISVs can provide this in several ways.

The simplest way, which allows users to make their own choices, is to permit customization via configuration. In this case, the user is offered a menu of selections and may make choices. For some products, these choices are made by a system administrator or Super User for all the users in a particularly role or category and the choices are not offered directly to the users themselves.

In other cases, the ISV may offer a set of APIs, describing the way in which a programmer may interface with the application. This permits a programmer to extend the application (in ways from simple to very sophisticated), but remain compatible and integrated with the SaaS application.

In the most sophisticated case, the ISV has written his application to a platform (his own or a third party) and the programmer (who may be another commercial ISV or a VAR, rather than internal IT staff) can write his own programs, substantially extending the function of the original program, but remaining compatible and capable of being integrated with it.

In both of these cases (APIs and a common platform), if the programmer obeys the rules, his extension or application should be able to remain compatible as upgrades are created and applied to the base SaaS program.

Is Customization Part of the SaaS Model?

In the ASP era (the predecessor to SaaS for web hosted applications), the conventional wisdom was that you couldn't permit hosted applications to be customized or support and upgrades would quickly become impossible to manage and uneconomical (that is, not profitable) for the ISVs who permitted this. There are still many SaaS providers who believe this. However, the popularity and success of ISVs like SalesForce.com who support extensive customization for both partners and users have made limited levels of customization much more popular.

If an application is for consumers or end users, it likely doesn't require customization beyond making choices as to the look of the interface and what kinds of data might be included or which other users can share the information.

For corporate users, more extensive customization, to better match their existing processes, might be appealing. In that case, the question becomes, "Who does what?" Customization might be performed by the ISV himself, as a kind of fee-paid consulting assignment. This can be all right (and a source of additional revenue) as long as it doesn't distract the ISV from his strategic path.

Often it's better to let partners do the customization – and to let them support the customized application, too. This provides them with an attractive revenue opportunity, while making the underlying application more appealing to potential customers. Of course, support for customized applications will need to be coordinated with support staff at the ISV who can sort out the tedious question of where a problem lies and help get it fixed.

Nowadays, when SaaS applications can often be extensively customized, yet continue to exploit new features in subsequent upgrades, and can be attached via standard API's to the customer's data bases and applications, it's much easier to make an argument for using SaaS for a variety of applications, particularly those that would be hard to justify supporting internally.

The relationship between SaaS and SOA

Many start-ups take advantage of SOA and use it as the architecture for their SaaS application. Traditional software ISVs moving to SaaS have the opportunity to address SOA and SaaS at the same time, decomposing their application into a set of services, and addressing the appropriate level of granularity issue as part of redesigning for SaaS. In that way, it may be possible to provide an improved environment for traditional customers while creating the SaaS version of their product. It is possible to port to SaaS without considering SOA, but it may be very late to take that step – sort of like buying a "new" car right before the model year change. It's new to you, but it looks old hat to everyone else.

ISVs are using SOA concepts (of creating applications from reusable, granular modules) to make it easy for them to make changes and additions as the marketplace makes its desires known. ISVs can use SOA in reworking their existing applications, or they can write a new application from scratch, using SOA concepts. In either case, they will save time and development resources and make future changes to the application easier. They will also be building in a new metaphor that makes it easier for other web services to be combined with their offering or to build new or custom services.

Investing in decomposing a traditional application into web services and using SOA to implement the SaaS application can be an excellent way to help create a rich, sophisticated application, that includes the depth of features often missing in new applications but which is easy to update when customer requirements demand new features.

BIPT is a vertical market ISV who employs IBM's SaaS platform to provide an insurance policy administration system for insurance carriers, both property and casualty, mainly for homeowners' insurance and mainly for Florida carriers. It is a net-native ISV.

The policy administration system is a cradle to grave system for insurance policies. Agents and producers use it to support their business, producing quotes, coverage information, and applications, supporting underwriting and making decisions as to whether to provide coverage. It can issue policies and endorsements, perform billing, manage policies and renewals, cancel policies for non-payment, add charges for needed changes in coverage and manage claims.

BIPT currently manages seven insurance carriers. They target small to mid-sized carriers who are more inclined to use a SaaS solution and who have little or no in-house IT infrastructure or the ability to administer complex systems. The carriers pay BIPT a license fee up front plus a set-up fee to digitize their rules and rates. They then pay a monthly fee based on the premiums being processed and the number of policies; all contracts are on a five-year basis. Their typical customer is small and outsources as much as possible; employees manage relationships, products, and marketing, not IT.

Marketing is obviously on a face-to-face basis. BIPT's small marketing department makes direct call based on leads generated by advertising in trade journals and trade shows. Their sales cycles are 6 to 12 months, with implementation taking 90 to 150 days, depending on customization needs. Most customers can meet 80% of their needs with the standard product. Because BIPT's offering is 100% web-based and they have SOA expertise in-house, they can handle a customer who wants to integrate a legacy application.

BIPT has been focusing on homeowner's insurance companies in Florida, identifying new carriers as they form. They find that larger companies are dipping their feet into the SaaS waters with a business unit and they are in talks with larger, multi-national companies about pilot programs.

Chapter 5. **The Cost of Changing to SaaS**

This chapter is for traditional ISVs changing to SaaS. Start-ups and customers may read it for context and background information, but the advice is not targeted to them.

If traditional ISVs could offer SaaS versions of their applications by simply pushing a button, more would do so sooner. But it's not just the task of getting the software to run smoothly in a hosted environment that must be considered. Offering a SaaS application means changing both the business model and the sales model, which will affect the entire business organization

Rewriting or Porting the Application vs. New Applications

Most ISVs consider this part of the change to SaaS first; in many ways it's the easiest task.

As we've noted earlier, ISVs need to choose between simply porting an existing application to a hosted environment, making the necessary changes to permit such SaaS requirements as self-service administration (you can't afford to add each new user and their IT department may not want that job) and whether to support multi-tenant use of the software.

Perhaps it should it be different, designed to exploit the web/hosted platform? Many traditional ISVs believe that any SaaS version will be acceptable and use platform-supported tools to move their application to SaaS without making any changes.

Of course, as we've noted earlier, traditional ISVs may find themselves competing with net native applications (new applications, written from the start for the web hosted environment). These applications will do a better job of exploiting the web environment and will be likely to emphasize new Web 2.0 features such as user participation (through the use of wikis and other collaborative features and mash-ups for instant integration) and richer interfaces (often through the use of AJAX).

This might work if the traditional ISV has a well-recognized brand and a demand for a SaaS version, at least for a time, but they may need to make further investments in developing a net-native SaaS version of their software as the market grows and becomes more competitive.

It then becomes a question of whether the traditional ISV's brand will be stronger than the new SaaS vendor's features.

The primary decision for an existing ISV is whether the SaaS application should complement or replace the existing traditional product. If the SaaS product is to replace the traditional product, the ISV must decide how long he will sell (and support) the older product, generally based on the size and commitment of its installed base and whether they are willing to move to the SaaS platform. If both versions will continue to be offered (more common), decisions must be made about how issues like pricing, features, and support will be rationalized across the products.

Changing the Business Model

In the SaaS business model, many things change. The trick is knowing in advance what the possibilities are and planning for something that the marketplace will support. A successful business model can almost always be found. There are companies, including some very young ones, who are making money in this strange new world because they made the right business decisions when they were getting started. Here are some of the things you will need to consider.

Changing Sources of Revenue

While traditional software companies get most of their revenue from the sale of software (and that up front, at the time of the sale), with some additional revenues from maintenance and support, consulting, and training, a SaaS software company has a different revenue picture.

Most of the revenue from a SaaS customer comes in through monthly subscription fees, over the life of the vendor/customer relationship. In some cases, it is possible to get the customer to sign an agreement to be a customer for some longer term – one, two, or three years – but many SaaS offerings are on a pure monthly contract, with customers coming and going at will; only the high quality of the software and the services behind it keep the revenues coming in. This means that until a SaaS vendor has a large portfolio of customers, all contributing their monthly subscription checks, revenue will be much less in the short run, although that will be eventually be made up by the continuing revenue stream.

For some SaaS applications, it is appropriate for the SaaS vendor to charge set-up fees. These pay for the cost of getting the customer's access to the application up and running and may include training some customer staff. They also help provide some up front revenue to the ISV. Some ISVs prefer to focus on their software and let business partners provide implementation and training.

Where appropriate, the SaaS vendor or a business partner may provide customization and/or integration services (such as integrating a customer data base or legacy application with the SaaS application). Such services are expected to be fee paid and represent another source of revenue. Customization shouldn't be undertaken lightly, to gain a particular customer. It should always be part of an overall strategy.

Changes in Operational Costs

When on-line software got started, many companies consisted of an idea, some software, and a server in someone's bedroom. Running a successful SaaS company takes a bit more infrastructure and support than that.

A few early SaaS companies went to the other extreme and built big data centers. In fact, they used these data centers as a selling point, implying that any SaaS vendor without his own data center couldn't possibly offer first class service. Don't believe it. SaaS vendors shouldn't spend their own capital building data centers. There is more data center space out there than you could possibly want and much of it is first class – state of the art hardware and software managed by world class talent. A small software vendor couldn't replicate it if he tried. A SaaS vendor needs to pick a good data center partner, remembering that the service this data center gives his customers will be how his product will be judged.

Part of picking a data center partner is deciding who is going to support what. Most data centers are just supporting the infrastructure (hardware, operating systems, performance, etc.). Supporting the application is usually the job of the SaaS ISV, although the data center might agree to provide first level support for a fee. It's also possible to offer premium support at a price, a good additional source of revenue, to customers who demand it. This is typically provided by the SaaS vendor, not the data center.

Part of this operational environment will be a billing system. ISVs need not create these themselves (although a few have). Several strong systems are available and several platform vendors offer a billing system as one of their platform services. The billing system will need to be flexible enough to allow you to provide any combination of users and usage your customers demand – billing by time, CPU usage, storage, transactions, etc.

Operational considerations should also be given to how much automation to incorporate. More is generally better. The system should be able to automatically provision customers, giving them preconfigured functions and features by roles, locations, systems, or other preferences. Automated provisioning allows the SaaS system to provide service and support to remote customers (in some sense every customer is a remote customer in a SaaS environment). A particularly good system would ultimately be able to integrate its provisioning and billing system with an existing IT function.

Cost of Migration (from Traditional SW Models)

When on-line software first began to appear in the late nineties, many ISVs thought it was an "all new customers" idea because the customers they already had would not be interested in hosted software. In fact, software vendors who offer SaaS versions of their existing products do see some cannibalization of their installed base. It's inevitable as some customers find that a hosted version of the software better suits their needs.

ISVs shouldn't try to avoid having this happen by punitive SaaS pricing, because that simply undermines their success in the SaaS market. Rather, they should be pleased that they are able to retain their customers as they move to a new software distribution and support model, rather than losing them to new SaaS competitors. The loss of revenue (if on-premises software carries a higher margin) should simply be considered a migration cost.

Another myth that still circulates is that SaaS business comes at little or no marketing cost. This simply isn't true. Business applications rarely succeed because of viral marketing (rapidly accelerating customer recommendations); business customers can't find your new SaaS software unless you tell them about it, which requires marketing.

Other Migration Costs

There are some things about a SaaS business which are very different than a traditional software business and which require some thinking and planning before getting very far into the SaaS implementation.

Business metrics will require a new way of looking at how your software business is doing: what to measure, what to compare it to (probably not your traditional software business), how to collect those measurements, how to amass comparative competitive data, and so forth. Eventually, you will want to compare traditional software to SaaS, but not until SaaS has been running for long enough (and has a large enough installed base and revenue stream) to make these comparisons valid.

Pipeline progression is how we tell how much business we're going to do this month or this quarter based on how much business is where in our sales management system. Once we have enough statistical data it is possible to know that we need $x worth of business booked four months ago to result in $x/2 worth of sales this month. In the beginning, it's necessary to determine whether you will be using the same system to book traditional and SaaS software (if you have both) and then to let the system run for a bit, trying to determine what it's telling you about the relationships between a new customer entering the system as an inquiry, various steps in the selling progress, and a completed sale, until it is possible to understand how to rely on the pipeline as a projection tool.

Cost of a Hybrid Business Model

One of the costs of moving to SaaS for a traditional software ISV is that you'll be running two businesses – your existing traditional software business and your new SaaS business. They will be quite different in many respects – revenue models, overhead costs, support requirements, and sales models.

How you will do this depends on what your goal is. If the plan is to keep right on selling your traditional software forever (or at least for the foreseeable future), you will need a model that anticipates balancing the two businesses and trying to predict what happens as the SaaS business grows.

If you believe the SaaS business will replace your traditional software business fairly quickly (read the case study on IT Factory for some insights), then you may need only plan how to tell your customers and prepare them for the change – and how to manage your cash flow so that you can fund your new business from the old one as you move over.

The ISV must also decide how he will alter or add to his sales channel to accommodate the need of his new SaaS product offering. Some ISVs sell both traditional and SaaS products through the same sales channels, offering their customers a choice. They still have to decide how to compensate their sellers (direct and indirect), given the different revenue patterns of SaaS products and how to incent salesmen to sell both products.

There is no question that it is easier to sell the SaaS product through its own (separate) channel and to acknowledge both products in both channels, referring appropriate sales across. This permits getting the right kind of sales organization (given that the SaaS organization may be much more heavily weighted toward webinars and telesales and the traditional software sales forces toward one-on-one selling), with the right compensation and incentives.

If the target customers for the SaaS product are the ISV's existing customers, the ISV will want to use existing relationships, branding, and ties to existing products to sell their SaaS product. But if the target customers are new customers (as, for example, when an enterprise software vendor chooses SaaS as a vehicle for selling to the SMB market), then much more effort will be required to form new relationships with customers who are not likely to be familiar with the vendor and his products and new channels will be required to reach these customers

On the other hand, some companies handle the dilemma of living in two worlds by simply doing it: they keep some of their business entirely on the traditional software model and move some particular part entirely to SaaS. Lawson has chosen to do that with their Recruitment software which is, over time, becoming a SaaS product. It's another form of hybridization.

Lawson is a traditional ISV with 4,000 customers in manufacturing, distribution, maintenance and service sector industries across 40 countries with solutions in Enterprise Performance Management, Supply Chain Management, Enterprise Resource Planning, Customer Relationship Management, Manufacturing Resource Planning, Enterprise Asset Management and vertical industry applications.

Lawson has taken some of their offerings in Human Capital Management to the SaaS platform and is also hosting some of their other applications for their customers in a single tenant environment. They have been decommissioning their old product for Recruiting and launched a new Integrated Talent Management in October, 2007.

Lawson has transitioned from a traditional software model for this product by internal development from scratch, using a Java-based infrastructure called Landmark to build the applications, suitable for both SaaS and on-premises deployment. Only the SaaS model is currently available. It is single tenant architecture, virtualized using IBM virtualization technology; this allows it support customization. Lawson will also give customers access to its Landmark tools.

Talent Management is sold on a three-year license, priced on a per employee per month basis and paid annually. It goes up and down based on employee counts and which of its seven modules (e.g., human resource record keeping, acquisition/recruiting, compensation, learning and development, succession management) are in use. Lawson has no plans to sell it on a credit card subscription, by the month, basis.

Lawson doesn't think of themselves as a platform; they're focused on capturing seats in the Talent Management market where they are narrowly focused. It's growing 15% a year and they will grow with both more customers and more modules.

Lawson sells Talent Management directly to both existing and new customers. Existing customers can generally be brought through a sales cycle in about 90 days; new customers take three to nine months, with some variability depending on vertical industry. This is not a traditional "everyone must have it" product, so they have a litmus test for selecting target customers. They find that a business has a need for more comprehensive talent management when it grows past 1,000 employees. It might be used in a smaller company where knowledge workers are the basis of the company's value, such as biotech.

They are considering using partners for implementation. They partner with IBM for middleware, including DB2 and WebSphere.

Chapter 6. Pricing

How to price for SaaS

Picking a price for a SaaS product can be tricky. Too many ISVs are inclined to look at competitive products and subtract a little. That makes you competitive, but it may not fit your business model – or your strategy of providing more service or a different mix of features.

The right price is the price that the customer will readily agree to pay. It's the price at which the value to the customer seems to match the price.

Keep in mind that what you charge for the similar (or identical) product in the traditional software market may not matter if you are facing a highly competitive situation in the SaaS market. On the other hand, if your product addresses a specialty market and is unlikely to see much competition, you can price accordingly – and you should.

Remember that applications aren't necessarily created equal and if you can make a strong case that what you're selling is more valuable to the buyers than what at first glance appears to be competitive, you may be able to support a higher price.

Long-term goals enter into pricing, too. If you're trying to become the market share leader, lower pricing can help you get there. Perhaps you will want to try a tiered pricing model, with a very low price for basic services, a somewhat higher price for what you hope most customers will buy, and premium pricing for optional but valuable add-ons. That way, you can target a broad market without pricing being an impediment and still hope to charge higher prices to customers who like what you have to sell and want to buy more.

A new SaaS ISV can start business with the SaaS subscription revenue model. He has to make this business model work, but he doesn't have to convert to the subscription model from an already successful (and possibly strongly entrenched) way of doing business. This is both an advantage and a disadvantage: on the plus side, there are no compromises to make, no decisions to avoid attracting existing customers; on the minus side there is no existing revenue stream which can help fund the new business and no existing brand or customer set which can help leverage the new SaaS business into being.

Existing ISVs, who are selling in the traditional software market, first need to decide whether they are changing to a SaaS business entirely or whether they are adding a SaaS offering to their existing business. Most pick the latter, although we will describe a company, IT Factory, who completely converted its business to SaaS.

In any case, the existing ISV will need to convert the SaaS part of their business to a subscription model, where revenue comes in continuously over time (and must for tax purposes be recognized that way) from a revenue model in which a great deal of revenue comes in up-front, with each new sale.

IT Factory was a traditional ISV that decided to change its strategy and become a SaaS ISV. While most ISVs in this situation look at SaaS as a complement to their existing strategy, IT Factory looked at it as a replacement strategy, with the goal of moving its entire installed base to the SaaS platform. (This has happened and they now have only 2% of their customers with an on-premise version of their software.)

IT Factory launched their PaaS to allow their business partners to enable their applications. They run as a single tenant solution to preserve maximum customizability. They believe that both their VARs and their user customers are sure that they require this customization to fit their special needs.

They originally SaaS-ified IBM and Microsoft developer tools and platforms including Java, .Net, Lotus Designer, and Visual Studio, hoping to get 5 ISVs to use them as a platform for their applications; instead they got 150 applications in 60 days. They have partnered with IBM to open a Lotus Store and a Blue Store for Cross-Brand IBM products; they intend to do this for other brands as well. This is a two-way street – it brings revenues to IT Factory and its business partners and it helps IBM to get more of its own revenues from SaaS without rewriting their applications (which are not themselves SaaS) and to continue to support customization.

They think of Microsoft, IBM, Oracle and SAP as the "final four," and wonder what to do about them in a world where SaaS is increasingly a software platform of choice. (Editorial Note: Of course, all of these vendors offer some SaaS solutions themselves; it is more a matter of how you get the customers exactly the combination of function and service they require, without having to leave their existing application investments behind.)

IT Factory thinks of SaaS as both a distribution vehicle and a pricing mechanism, but they feel the pricing mechanism is not required. As they say, who would say no to saving money and avoiding implementation and ongoing management problems but having the same quality as before?

With so many existing customers moving over, IT Factory already has hundreds of thousands of seats on their PaaS platform and more than 100 partners. They have ambitious targets for 2010 where they are looking for 1,000 business partners, 1,000 SaaS-ified applications and 3,000 systems administrators and business partners for IBM products with more than 200 users in large accounts (more than 5,000 work stations) plus 300 mid market accounts (more than 1,000 work stations). They have had to be a bit cautious about not taking on very large customers until they and/or their partners have the bandwidth to handle them.

Their business model revolves around selling through partners, but very large enterprises could be partners themselves, with their own IT staff. Not surprisingly, their marketing plan is all about signing up new partners. They claim they can sign up business partners in as little as 24 hours and a customer in as little as 3 to 6 weeks (with a business partner). Subscriptions are open-ended and do not require long-term commitments, just a 30-day minimum, but there are discounts for longer periods. Customers can take the discount up front but then back out and pay back the discount if they change their mind.

Last year we wrote about IT Factory's unique solution to their migration from traditional ISV to PaaS; they partnered with IBM Global Financial Services. IT Factory provided the services and customers signed contracts with IBM GFS directly for the agreed upon time period, with the net present value of the contract being paid up front to IT Factory, giving them the funds to make the migration. IBM was more than happy to talk about this and to assure us that for another mature, stable IBM partner moving to SaaS, with customers who are willing to sign appropriate contracts, they'd be willing to consider doing this again.

None of this answers two compelling issues:

1. **Long-term commitments:** In fact, while SaaS contracts are calculated as subscription contracts, most of them (with the exception of consumer and very small business software) are booked as one to five year contracts, with

discount incentives for longer contracts. This means that while it is theoretically possible to change from one SaaS vendor to another, it is less likely to occur. The flexibility of the subscription model is generally exercised in a more granular way; subscribers are encouraged to add subscribers and software modules during the term of the contract and may be permitted to drop subscribers and modules on the annual renewal dates.

2. **License Ownership:** The ownership of SaaS licenses is a murky issue. If I pay a subscription fee for a one-year license for a SaaS software product, at the end of the year I don't own anything but my data and it isn't clear I could do anything with it without the software. Some aggregators are allowed to buy licenses directly from SaaS software vendors to use on behalf of all of their customers; other SaaS software vendors require that each customer buy his own licenses (in that case it does seem that the customer owns the licenses).

Billing

Billing for SaaS vendors is done in so many different ways that it is not yet possible to say that there is a standard technique. The ISV can have his own billing system; the platform vendor can provide one; the platform vendor can use one from a billing provider (another SaaS vendor) or the ISV can make his own arrangements with a billing software vendor. All this is wending its way toward an arrangement where billing becomes part of the platform offering but is provided by a billing expert company.

The billing models have become increasingly complex so that now one can bill for nearly anything, however granular or obscure.

Aria Systems provides on-demand billing and customer

lifecycle management solutions. Their solutions are generally provided to platform companies and telcos as well as to individual ISVs. Aria focuses on specificity and flexibility, allowing its customers to offer a nearly infinite number of different plans. This allows different types of providers to bill differently, a multi-tier channel to provide segmented tracking and billing, and a complex market (like telecommunications) to offer many subtly different plans to customers. Aria can bill for indirect channels, manage many levels of usage and sub-usage for applications such as gaming, and record credits towards awards for customer loyalty programs and gaming, in real time.

Aria has been offering its services for nearly five years and currently has 55 customers; about one-third are full-spectrum users, taking advantage of both Aria's billing and its customer management services. Rather than counting customers, they think of their growth in terms of invoices generated. More than 6 million invoices were generated in the first half of 2008, growing from 1.2 million in 2007 as customers went from dipping their toes to actual use. Aria also added some very large users in the data center and health care business.

These customers pay Aria based on revenue, with some base level guarantees at the beginning, plus some fees for implementation, professional services as needed, customization, and business intelligence.

Aria markets partly through very good PR, engaging industry analysts and the trade press; they believe at this stage of the market, many companies are getting their information from these sources. They also do direct marketing, especially for the larger deals with customers who will be using their product for their own large customer base. Sales cycles vary greatly – from as little as a few weeks for small ISVs to as long as 6 months or more for a large enterprise. While they market their services through partners, they are handling implementation and customization themselves for now. Of course, they will use more partners such as the platform providers and move out into the mid-size enterprises with the SaaS industry as they replace traditional legacy systems, particularly in vertical markets.

Note the layering effect: Aria concentrates on billing, letting the ISV concentrate on the application. Expect to see more of this layering as the SaaS market matures.

ISSUES FOR CUSTOMERS

Chapter 7. Customer Expectations

Who Uses SaaS?

It is a computing industry myth that SaaS is appealing only or mainly to consumers and the SMB market. The myth's origins are easy to trace. In the early days of the ASP market, traditional software vendors wanted to downplay the importance of on-line software. They either ignored it entirely or considered it a possible complement to their existing business, a way to sell to the SMB market without disturbing their current and lucrative enterprise and mid-market customers.

In fact, from the very start, on-line software has appealed to customers in companies of every size. It is particularly appealing to users who can not get that kind of functionality quickly and easily – if at all – either because they do not have the resources of an IT department or because their IT department cannot give their needs an appropriate priority.

The chart on Who Will Use SaaS sums up the issues. In large enterprises, SaaS will not be used (at least not yet) for mission critical applications. But it will be used to support remote locations and users, infrequently used and specialty applications, and applications that are shared with outsiders – contractors, consultants, suppliers, customers – whom IT prefers not to permit inside the firewall. SaaS will often be challenged as unable to provide a suitable level of service, or to support integration with internal applications, or the level of customization large enterprises prefer. All of these challenges can be met, but perhaps not at a level that a large enterprise would find satisfactory.

In the SMB market, SaaS provides a way for organizations to have access to applications that they would otherwise not be able to implement and support, because SaaS provides not just software, but implemented software, managed and supported. It allows the SMB to compete more equally in the marketplace with larger firms. And, of course, it offers his organization the same advantages for remote and external users that it offers larger firms. For SMBs, the challenges are in selecting vendors, since they will often need to do this with less formal assistance than customers in large enterprises who can use their IT department as advisers. They will also have to deal with integrating multiple SaaS applications and with the problem of predicting costs in an environment where one is billed on a usage basis.

Individual users often are very loyal SaaS users, especially since many SaaS products are free or very inexpensive in their individual versions. SaaS vendors often hope to use these individual professional users as advocates, helping to sell larger installations of their products over time. They will, of course, not get much support, since individual SaaS software is often offered with minimal support, so caution should be taken in selecting a reliable vendor and care taken in using it for serious business work. A user might, for example, want to keep off-line copies of his files.

Who Will Use SaaS		
Organization/User	**Type of Use**	**Challenges**
Large Enterprises	Non-Mission Critical Applications Remote Locations and Users Infrequently Used Applications Applications Shared with non-Employees	Level of Service Application Integration Customization
SMBs	Large Scale Applications Support of Remote Locations and Users Applications Shared with non-Employees	Vendor Selections Application Integration Complex, Unpredictable Bills
Individual Professional Workers	Multi-Location Work Shared Applications	Identifying Reliable Vendor Application Integration

What Do Customers Want?

Customers are drawn to SaaS for a number of reasons, of which cost savings is often mentioned, but rarely first. What customers are looking for is easy access to function, and access as quickly as possible. SaaS is particularly appealing when compared to conventional software with its long decision process, followed by a lengthy design and implementation process. Many SaaS products which can be accessed immediately (within an hour) would take weeks or more to set up as an internal application. More complex applications that would take a few weeks or a month to implement in a SaaS environment, (mainly for formatting and connecting data), might take months to a year or more in a traditional software environment.

The issues most often mentioned for considering SaaS include:

- **Cost Savings** - A tricky issue. Customers often try to compare the subscription fees from a SaaS vendor to the cost of a software package, forgetting that a software package requires hardware, perhaps additional complementary software, and IT resources to implement, manage, and support it. All those are included in the SaaS offering, so the prospective buyer must calculate those costs, too, to get an accurate comparison. Remember, too, that customers need SaaS vendors to make an appropriate profit to continue to invest in their service and have an incentive to stay in business – otherwise customers will be in for an unpleasant surprise!

- **Faster Time to Value** – This is perhaps the best incentive for using SaaS. It's already there, waiting for the customer to use it now. Implementation time is minimal, ranging from minutes to weeks, allowing customers to get on with their projects and reap the benefits of collaboration, project management, sales campaigns, or whatever the SaaS software provides without weeks or months of waiting, to say nothing of the uncertainty of whether the implemented application will actually match customer expectations. In SaaS it should be right there for the customer to see and try; it works or it doesn't work. Of course, modifications are sometimes possible (see Customization), but what the software does and whether it matches the customer's needs should be quickly apparent.

- **Skill Savings** – When customers buy an application from a SaaS source rather than via the traditional software route, the skill to implement, manage, and support the software is supplied by the SaaS vendor. This allows customers with small or no IT departments to more readily use complex, sophisticated applications, perhaps with some fee-for-services help from either the ISV or a third party. Larger customers can conserve their IT resources for mission critical applications by judiciously employing some SaaS applications in their IT mix. This is particularly important when a technology or philosophy change is sweeping through the IT industry, since trained and experienced staff in the new skill sets will be very scarce until the new techniques have had a chance to settle in.

- **Support for Remote Workers** – Many companies use SaaS entirely to be able to support an increasingly geographically distributed work force. This can be as simple as more employees working from home or as complex as workers spread out across the globe. For many companies, projects are not completed just by employees, but rather by teams which might include employees, suppliers, customers, and consultants, working across locations and time zones. A shared space, with shared supporting applications, becomes a critical part of getting work successfully completed. That is one reason why so much SaaS software, regardless of which vertical industry it's directed towards, is likely to include collaborative elements.

- **Support for non-Mission Critical Tasks** – Many enterprise CIOs tell me that they're not ready to place their mission critical tasks or data on SaaS infrastructures; they're concerned about issues like security and data integrity. In fact, a well run SaaS vendor with an impeccably run professional data center partner behind him might well offer more security and data integrity than all but the best-run IT shops, but we'll save that argument for another day, because the CIOs are ready, it's clear, to move some of their non-mission critical tasks to SaaS. Which tasks varies from company to company, but frequently named applications include HR, electronic mail, and collaboration, as well as specialized applications that are only used by small groups of users.

Southern Oak Insurance Company is a residential property insurance company located in Florida and started in 2004. It was looking for systems to handle processing for its agents and its claims. They looked at BIPT's TIVA System (discussed elsewhere in this book) because it is used by other insurers in its market and its agents were already familiar with it. The system allows 24/7 access anywhere in the world and allows Southern Oaks to give its business partners immediate access to the systems with appropriate authority levels.

Southern Oaks started using the BIPT system in early 2005 with 1,000 to 1,500 independent agents and 40 internal users; today there are about 4,500 users. Originally, BIPT offered Southern Oaks a 3-year agreement with a one-time license fee plus a storage fee based on the premium dollars and a volume discount. They are also charging a set-up fee and an annual maintenance fee. Custom programming is charged separately and performed by BIPT; Southern Oaks has done quite a bit of that to meet government regulations. Now they renew their contract on a year-to-year basis. The BIPT software is integrated with their claims system for data exchange and their accounting software.

BIPT has done a good job in Southern Oaks' estimation. The system has had almost no downtime and has done a good job at rating properly. Of course, there are always things that could be prettier such as when the underwriter is looking at risk, there could be an easier way to see claims without exiting his current position, via a better interface and higher level of integration. One of the issues is that BIPT has multiple customers and everyone wants something slightly different, so there are some compromises.

Southern Oaks uses other SaaS products, which made it more willing to try the BIPT product; their staff had also had some experience with BIPT's previous in-house software in other organizations. They did look at some competitive products which they thought might be more flexible, but they were concerned about the stability of the rating engine. BIPT was selected as the most stable environment.

Chapter 8. Challenges and Choices

Integration – Nearly every company, regardless of size, has existing applications. That means SaaS applications may have to connect to some of these applications to optimize the flow of information and work. Many SaaS applications are now capable of connecting to "legacy" (existing) applications through the SaaS application's APIs or through connectors written for specific applications (this works best if you have a mainstream application with few customizations). Of course, the more integration a firm needs between SaaS applications or between SaaS applications and legacy applications, the more time it will take to get everything just right and the more skilled labor will be required to connect everything together.

It is worth noting that SOA is often helpful here, on multiple dimensions. First, wrapping legacy applications in SOA may make it easier to connect them to SaaS applications. Secondly, if you are in the process of considering moving to SOA architectures for some of your more important existing applications, you can consider how to use SOA to connect them to the SaaS applications you are planning to use. Third, many SaaS applications use SOA methodologies which you may be able to tap into in implementing your integration strategy.

Webalo is an eight-year-old firm that helps companies take their information and make it available on mobile devices so that mobile executives can quickly make business decisions. It is particularly interesting because it's using SOA to deliver a SaaS solution. Webalo is not an application, but rather a platform that sits between users and their devices and the applications and data they need to access.

At a 300-store retail jewelry chain the executives get information on inventory, sales, and other necessary data on their mobile devices, provided as a service by Webalo. The service is all about simplicity. It can be offered hosted or it can be provided on the customer's site on a Webalo appliance, in which case it will still be a supported service, pushing or pulling updates (as desired) to the user devices.

The service supports a range of tools for administration plus a client piece which supports devices for off-line function, including a generated interface for the device. Wizards help the administrators get the applications and data connected to the user devices.

An early version of the application is in full production; a second version will become available shortly. At first, Webalo only supported business intelligence (BI) data; now it is opening up to more data sources such as web sites, web services, and other data bases. Webalo can federate data across a number of resources. About 30 customers are live on this early version of the service, mainly mid-size companies, especially in the retail and financial services sectors. Webalo expects that the service will be popular in its appliance form with larger firms such as larger banks and F500 companies. Many large firms want to innovate new uses of tech knowledge on a limited basis in tough economic times and then come out quickly as the economy improves, in a very competitive position.

The product is priced in a traditional subscription model, starting at $25 per user per month, discounted when users get to an annual fee at volume. Most organizations start with a pilot for a few users on a monthly basis and then move onto a hundred or more users on an annual contract.

Although Webalo can sell directly, they expect that they will make many of their sales through partners in the telco industry and other partners.

Their big advantage is simplicity; they can move access to the mobile devices without the need for programming.

Customization is an issue of where you are willing to compromise. Some organizations have committed to trying to run off-the-shelf software with no customizations beyond menu-based configuration choices. They will save a lot of money and time but give up some choice. Other organizations will feel it is worth the price in dollars and time to have an application look and behave exactly the way they want it to; they should keep in mind these are not only up-front costs, but also substantial on-going costs that must be paid every time the ISV updates the software and customizations must be redone to accept the update.

Some SaaS ISVs try to offer a best of both worlds approach, offering customization to both their partners and to internal IT via APIs and tools. These customizations will ride on top of future upgrades without the need to be rewritten, but they are, of course, limited by the rules of the API environment.

Picking the Right Vendor might be the single most important task for a customer who is deciding to use a SaaS application. Customers should look for a vendor who not only has a compelling application with the right functions, but also a vendor with an excellent reputation for service and support. This includes knowing something about the extent and robustness of their infrastructure (it's best that there be at least two locations, with your data and applications backed up so that an outage on one is invisible to users), and whether they own it or whether they use well-respected third party infrastructure players (better). Customers above the individual user level should also seek a SLA (Service Level Agreement), where the SaaS vendor sets out what penalties will be available to the customers should agreed upon service levels (performance, up-time) not be met. Any serious forays into SaaS demand that customers require references from existing customers, preferably customers of a similar size, using similar services. Check them out. It's also wise to do a little web searching to see if the vendor's reputation seems to survive the forums and communities boards where disgruntled customers air their gripes. A bit of this can be overlooked, but a tsunami should require an adequate explanation.

Standards

Some SaaS vendors are as proprietary as any traditional software vendor. Others are devoted to industry standards. Until we have strong standards for data and applications in the SaaS space that make it easy to move from one vendor to another, taking your data with you, it's wise to be aware of exactly what you're getting into. If you're putting a large enterprise's email system into a proprietary set-up, you should make sure that it's widely available elsewhere or that the code can be escrowed on your behalf and updated on a regular basis, to protect your interests. You should also see how you are going to update your data (outside the SaaS vendor's system) on a regular basis. SaaS doesn't change the rules of wise IT management; it just changes where computing is done.

Don't pick a SaaS vendor on price alone. If your SaaS vendor isn't making a profit, he will not be able to provide good support or to improve the software (if it is his own). A good vendor is one that will endure and to endure he must make a reasonable profit. Keep that in the selection equation.

THE FUTURE OF SAAS

The story of SaaS has scarcely begun; its future is mainly ahead. Today we are moving from a period in which SaaS was a novelty, an experiment for brave individuals and organizations, to a period in which SaaS is becoming a mainstream solution.

As with any technology, it is not likely to be the solution for everything, but rather the best solution for many things. Using it successfully means selecting the best places to implement SaaS and the best places to continue to use other technologies. It also means continuously examining SaaS and its underpinnings to pair it with newly developing technologies and to refine SaaS offerings, as well as the way in which SaaS is combined with other (legacy) offerings and the user experience SaaS applications can provide.

Along the way, there are some questions we expect customers and ISVs to encounter. In some cases, we believe the answers are already known; in others, the market will have to determine them over time. Knowing the questions, however, will help market participants plan more knowledgably for their success.

Chapter 9. Customer Trends

Will customers expect to buy all their SaaS applications from a single provider?

As the SaaS market started, each ISV offered its own SaaS application, sometimes on its own platform, sometimes with the partnership of a platform provider. But customers are unlikely to want to manage individual relationships with dozens (or hundreds) of individual ISVs, even for billing purposes, much less for support and integration. There is also the issue of how individual users might be provisioned for just the applications the organization wants to provide them with, selecting from the dozens it has contracted for, and how users navigate their way among dozens of different interfaces and semantics.

We suspect there are several possible answers here.

(1) In the short run, aggregators will select the best applications (in their opinion) and offer them as a portfolio to their customers. Customers will be able to select which applications to use and provision different individuals in their organization with sub-sets of their selection. The aggregators will provide first-level support and will provide some assistance with higher levels of support. They will also be responsible for some well-defined levels of integration, especially the ability to pass data between applications. For a few aggregators and their customers, this is already true today. (See *JamCracker.*)

(2) Over time, some platform vendors (PaaS) will establish an ecosystem of applications for their platform. In some cases, they will behave like aggregators, offering to market

and support the entire portfolio. In other cases, they will behave as Salesforce.com does today, offering ecosystem partners participation in a loose federation where their applications can integrate and interoperate with other applications on the platform (via stated APIs) but will be marketed and supported separately by the individual ISVs. In some SaaS markets (for example verticals like Life Insurance or Patient Care) it is entirely possible that a single platform provider will be the force behind a strong cluster of applications, making it hard for others to compete in that market.

NetSuite is a very visible vendor with a portfolio of applications intended to be a full suite for the mid-market, for firms from 10 to 1,000 employees, offering applications from web contact to CRM to Inventory management to Sales Financials. Their goal is to offer a complete solution with everything integrated.

This SaaS ISV started out as a mini-Oracle offering (it is mainly owned by Oracle's founder and leader Larry Ellison), but it has since severed its relationship with Oracle and become a separate company.

NetSuite's sweet spot has been the 250 employee-size company; in larger organizations it is more likely that NetSuite is used as a spot solution in a department. However, they have been moving up market, recently adding in-house consulting and support capabilities that allow them to serve larger firms directly. Today, the company has about 5,600 companies as customers and about 1 million unique log-ins or "seats."

Customers normally sign a minimum one year contract, although some prefer to lease and pay once a year. There is no required up-front fee; initial implementation work can be performed by NetSuite, a partner, or the customer themselves. Customers pay a base fee plus a per user fee;

users may be added during a contract but they may not be subtracted except at renewal.

NetSuite primarily markets its products directly but has a reseller channel for both sales and implementation. About 80% of sales are by NetSuite directly; about 20% are through partners. The sales cycle runs about 45 days, on average.

NetSuite has been encouraging its partners to provide customizations on top of its base products. That could be as simple as changing labels and formats or extending the data base structure or more complex projects such as changing work flow, using SuiteScript (their JavaScript) to enforce business rules. NetSuite has designed their product so that properly written customizations ride on top and do not break when an upgrade occurs. NetSuite upgrades about twice a year. They could do so more often, but their customers prefer not to have change occur too frequently.

NetSuite competes with CRM vendors like Salesforce.com and Siebel and accounting vendors such as Sage, Great Plains, SAP, and ACCPAC.

Here is a vendor that is simultaneously expanding its portfolio, expanding the services it provides (more consulting) and moving up market. If it succeeds it could prove to be a strong competitor in their market category.

(3) If standards are established in the SaaS market, making it easy for users to move from one application to another and developers to integrate across applications and platforms, aggregation may become much simpler. It might become something offered by portal vendors, with SaaS applications plugging into their user interface environments and being provisioned via their policy engines. Or a separate layer of players could evolve, responsible for user interfaces, integration, and support.

(4) We would expect that some larger ISVs, aggregators, and PaaSs would become portfolio players over time, acquiring additional applications via acquisition. This is a market with many small players and a few big ones, and software is a market where there is a natural tendency for a few large players to occupy most (80-90%) of any category. It is easier in SaaS markets for small players to reach their market and service their customers, but it is also easy for large vendors to integrate them with their portfolio offerings. The market is always likely to be full of young, small companies, but it is also likely to have many small companies who are acquired into larger firms to expand their portfolios and market share. This process is already going on.

Global Groupware Solutions is an Indian SaaS ISV who moved from a traditional CRM product to a SaaS CRM product in 2001 and then developed a more sophisticated multi-tenancy ERM (Employment Management) SaaS product in 2007, which is now the focus of the company's business.

SmileERM is designed to meet SaaS expectations with low price points and the ability to integrate with data and other applications. This requires multi-tenancy. They allow customers to do benchmarking, including competitive comparisons, anonymously. Global's CEO Sumeet Kapur believes that in areas where standardization is possible, multi-tenancy will be the rule; in areas where each company is unique, single tenancy will continue to accommodate full customization.

Kapur is certain that with SaaS, India can enter the product space as well as the service space (where they are already well established). The economics change completely here because SaaS is about IP creation and delivery is low cost. He believe Indians will be able to write software that is appropriate for different locations – to handle compliance issues, for example

– but managing developer talent will be about the same as it is everywhere (and we'd note that the price of skilled developers has been steadily increasing in India).

SaaS software can be designed to facilitate customers deploying it worldwide. For example, names/labels can be made easily changed (name vs. position vs. title); customers can be provided with an interface that allows them to easily make changes. Of course, not every situation is the same. Some industries are global; others are local and change by geography. Some applications require domain expertise for specific areas; others are more generic and simply require computer skills.

Global's customers (about 3,500 seats for an application that is just getting started) are divided evenly between multinationals operating in India and Indian companies using SmileERM in India. Their next step will be to sell it to multinationals operating outside of India.

SmileERM is sold on a subscription model of a fee per user per month. There is no up-front charge other than a nominal implementation charge. Eight modules are included in this fee, making the application less complex to use and the cost more predictable.

SmileERM is sold through direct sales to mid-market and enterprise customers. The company tried a web-only sales model but found it was inappropriate for these larger firms which require a discussion of process automation. It normally takes three to six months to close a sale. Global works with several partners for sales and intends to also have implementation partners. Their partner qualifications have changed from Systems Integrators with technical knowledge to consultants with domain expertise.

Global is an excellent example of a pure SaaS vendor in an

emerging country and its software markets. They must compete with traditional software vendors (such as Lawson and PeopleSoft) as well as SaaS vendors like Workday. But they will focus on ERM where they want to be best of breed whereas Workday is looking to have a much broader portfolio and aim higher in the enterprise. They note that smaller US SaaS companies don't tend to go global until they get to $100 million in revenue and then they tend to head for the UK and Europe first; that will give them lots of time and space to grow.

Global wants to focus on finding an implementation model for the SMB space, so that they can take advantage of SaaS making application software more affordable, eliminating the need for capital and significantly minimizing the need for IT skills. It takes the typical on-premises ISV implementation model which is non-scalable, built around human services, with quality going down as volume goes up, and stands it on its head. The challenge for SaaS is to eliminate implementation to the point where anybody can use the service without any assistant, with the defaults built in and the choices easily accessible.

In the final analysis, the company that adds value to the product and carries it into the customer environment might be a telco or a bank, providing integration with other service companies to provide travel services, recruiting, concierge services (find a birthday present or a restaurant reservation), all at a price your credit line can afford.

Bringing SaaS In-House

Many large enterprises are reluctant to use SaaS for important applications or to have mission critical data stored outside of their own premises. Recently, a number of them have begun looking at SaaS (which many use for limited applications, non-essential tasks, or remote users) to assess whether they should consider implementing the SaaS architecture internally for their own future application development.

This would permit them to provide centralized application management and support to their users while continuing to maintain control of their computing environment. To some it seems to be the best of both worlds. Some companies want to simply bring SaaS applications they like inside their own firewall – and many SaaS ISVs are perfectly willing to cooperate with this effort. Other enterprises want to architect their own future applications using SaaS methodology, making it easy to provision users, promulgate updates and patches, and make more efficient use of resources. Still others want to take existing legacy applications and combine them with third party SaaS applications in an environment that will look seamless and inviting to their users.

This mixed model (SaaS and on-premise solutions) can be solved in a number of ways. It can be solved by putting the SaaS applications on premise, but it can also be solved by integrating SaaS applications running in the cloud with legacy applications running inside the enterprise's firewall (with the right security and connectivity solutions supporting integration). There is also the "half-way house" solution we mentioned earlier, placing an appliance with the SaaS solution inside the firewall, but managing and supporting it from the SaaS vendor's premises. In that way, all the applications and data are on the customer's premises, but the customer has less responsibility for managing the SaaS application.

How this will work depends a great deal on what the customer wants. Enterprises with vast IT resources and a need for control (see the TransUnion story) will pick a very different solution than a smaller firm that simply wants to run more sophisticated software, integrated with its existing applications, without having to add to its internal IT resources.

TransUnion is one of the three giant credit bureaus that control all of our lives. Literally. They collect information on our assets, our liabilities, and how we pay our bills, and make that information available to their business subscribers so they can decide whether to grant us mortgages, credit cards, or loans and on what terms. Businesses can decrease risk by asking to see only customers with certain demographics (salaries, home ownership, debt to credit ratio, whatever) and customers can insure their credit health by periodically checking to see that only correct information is in their file.

To do this, TransUnion has been collecting information since 1968 and has more than 3100 employees in 25 countries on five continents.

TransUnion does use SaaS now for applications like Human Resources and ERP, but that's about 2% of their data processing. IT is, after all, what they do for a business and they are in a regulated industry where they have to protect their information by law, which constrains things. Their CIO says he'd be more than willing to use someone else's compute cycles and storage, but he'd need them to provide unlimited liability and no one is ready to sign up for that – yet. Some service providers say they could do that, but TransUnion is talking about everyone in the United States, perhaps 190 million people and no one can do that. "The platform technologies we're being offered are not yet robust enough to isolate and protect our data and compute cycles."

The bottom line is that TransUnion is so big that hosting their stuff with a service provider isn't more economical than what they can do themselves. They can use it for non-critical stuff; they use Salesforce.com and might consider Workday (Human Resources), but the issue is the main credit data base and the products associated with it which is 98% of TransUnion's computing.

TransUnion notes that they are a SaaS provider for their customers. When someone goes to open a bank account for a Citigroup customer, they access credit data information about that customer in making their decision that he is who he claims to be and that he's someone they want to have as a banking customer. They also consume data from SaaS providers, such as address verification information from Pitney-Bowes Finalist system.

It's really an issue of the business model. It gets in the way of what could be done. If this were a public good instead of a profit making company, it might be different. One could make the SaaS application as robust as it needed to be and not care what it cost. That's not an option in the for-profit world; we have to consider cost. There are other issues. People can make mistakes. There are unintentional consequences. No one can test for everything. The company tolerates a certain amount of business risk to get things to market in real time.

So what should be different to let them use the cloud? They could focus on the network issues and offer different levels of networking ranging from a private network, to VPNs over the Internet to the Internet itself. Customers could choose what to sign up for and pay for their choice.

The problem is the architecture of the Internet. There are three providers in the credit bureau industry – TransUnion, Equifax, and Experian – one of them should always be available and they all provide equivalent services. But no one can write an SLA for an internet customer because the latency is too variable and when a credit bureau loses a customer due to failure they don't lose him for a transaction or a day, they generally lose him for a month. A two-tier Internet scheme might help, but probably not very much. There is tiered service available now but it's not granular enough for this situation.

For now, TransUnion is unlikely to outsource their main credit information application, but they might move to an internal SaaS architecture for themselves and they will be likely to offer more SaaS applications to their customers.

A Better User Experience

It would not be at all surprising if in five years the major SaaS vendors were content experts (on various business matters such as credit, insurability, healthcare issues, and federal regulations, for example) plus some number of aggregators who put together collections of software for the portals through which the applications were delivered.

Users would probably receive their services through one or two portals (perhaps a business portal and a personal one). Inside each portal, all the applications would be aggregated, pulled through a single user interface, and able to access all of the user's data.

The user would care not at all who made the software or how that happened. In the business world, someone (probably the IT department) would select the user's portfolio, perhaps permitting some choices; in the personal world, the user would make her own choices, the most important being which portal to choose, since that would determine which services would be available.

Who will those portal vendors be? That is not yet determined. They might be the platform vendors of today – Salesforce and Microsoft, IBM and Google; or they might be huge aggregators of customer relationships – the telcos and cable companies, the banks and credit card companies, buying branded portals and portfolios of services from the technology vendors, but finding a new level of relationship with their customers.

In each vertical sector we are likely to find a cluster of SaaS companies, some providing technical expertise, others subject matter experts, together providing all the services and infrastructure that a company in that sector requires to do business. Perhaps these verticals will provide horizontal tools (HR, ERP, etc.) for complete software portfolios or perhaps they will be sold as part of a vertical offering by a large horizontal vendor who is himself a platform and portal provider.

Anything is possible. Everything can be connected.

Chapter 10. Technology Trends

Cloud Computing

Originally, Cloud Computing was a vague term for a very vague and distant future in which computing would occur in a few remote locations without the need for very much human intervention. Infinite computing resources would be available for any need at costs approaching zero. Certainly, users would not need to know or care about how the computers, their software, or the network functioned.

In the real world, physical computing progressed differently. We cycled between periods when computing was more centralized (and seemed more remote and less accessible to users) and other periods when computing was right on user desktops. No one was ever satisfied. Centralized computing failed to give users enough control and was too inflexible. Distributed computing made every user his own system administrator and was very inefficient.

In the last few years, as the cost of a unit of computing power has continued to decrease – but the cost of humans with the skills to implement and manage computer systems has not – the vision of centralized computing has returned. It has taken several turns. Some computer scientists have suggested (and experimented with) a vast Grid of computers, attached via the Internet, whose power can be combined for large-scale tasks when needed. In some cases, very large computing systems can be part of these grids for specialized tasks. Others have suggested a computing Utility which would provide just as much computing power as an organization needed, on an on-demand basis, much like electricity.

Eventually, as large web users such as Google and Amazon built out enormous data centers for their own purposes, they realized that they could permit others to access these "clouds" of computing power at relatively attractive prices. The Cloud computing era began.

Today, many companies are putting together very large data centers, sometimes as extensions of their own needs, sometimes just for customers to use. Originally the idea was that these clouds of computing would offer processing power and storage. Anything else would be added by the customer. As the idea became more popular, additional function has been added. Some clouds also offer systems management. Others are actually providing a set of applications as part of the cloud.

We could be grammarians and complain that applications are not supposed to be part of the cloud's vocabulary, but the market will sort this out. For now, most buyers think that cloud computing means compute resources on-demand, perhaps including applications, delivered over the Internet.

A Cloud of One's Own

For most organizations, a decision on cloud computing will be a matter of choosing which cloud to use. (Many may use several, selecting different clouds for different purposes.)

But for some large enterprises and government organizations, a cloud of their own may be an appropriate solution. IBM is already offering to build user-specific clouds and has had several takers, including Wuxi City of China to support new entrepreneurs, the Vietnamese government institutions and universities to energize innovation in their country, and iTricity, a utility-based hosting service provider headquartered in the Netherlands. Sogeti, part of global consulting firm Capgemini, has bought their own cloud to help them transform their company culture and move people into a Web 2.0 environment. Softex of Brazil will use its cloud to accelerate its software industry.

This allows the organization to optimize the cloud for its own purposes and to make it available to its own constituency. In the future, we would not be surprised to see some very large enterprises with clouds of their own and some systems integrators who maintain clouds to service their customers' needs.

Convergence of SaaS and SOA

How do SOA and SaaS converge and what are the consequences?

Writing new SaaS applications and moving existing software to the SaaS platform both require thinking through software architectures and writing code, in some cases writing extensive new code. SOA is a methodology and an architecture that allows software to be written as a series of granular services. If an existing application has already been written as a SOA application, it may be much easier to port it to a SaaS environment with minimum rewriting. If a vendor is writing a new application or extensively reworking an existing one (whether that is for a SaaS port or for other purposes), considering how using SOA will permit repurposing the proposed work for SaaS can offer future advantages in faster changes or economical repurposing.

CONCLUSIONS

SaaS is at the beginning of its journey. We can expect it to be around for many years, but to change and evolve continuously throughout its life cycle. What else could one expect from a technology whose central promise is that it can deliver a new, upgraded version several times a year without expecting users to do anything but enjoy the new features that are now offered?

Every time I read an article about SaaS I discover yet another acronym[3] (some of them last, some of them quickly disappear), as vendors, the press, and analysts try to get their hands around this very dynamic market.

SaaS is mainstream now. Customers of every size, from SMB to the largest enterprise, are using SaaS for some of their applications. Popular applications are HR, CRM, and Email. We expect to see a lot of collaboration and other social computing applications moving to SaaS as well as many vertical market applications. But anything is fair game and we have seen software vendors try everything from retail inventory to sausage factory management.

Expect everything about SaaS to change: the vendors, their market shares, the way applications are delivered, their prices.

- We expect many more traditional software firms to enter the SaaS market and some of them to succeed.

- Many firms we have never heard or dreamed of will invent themselves and a few will succeed beyond their wildest dreams, perhaps inventing new ways of doing things in the process.

- The software will disappear into the service and few users

---

[3] The latest I've seen is Xaas for "Anything as a Service," intended to suggest what might be delivered in the cloud.

will think of it as software anymore, just as you don't think of software when you order concert tickets from Ticketmaster or a movie from Netflix. (That makes it harder to charge for "software.")

- Pricing will go to transaction pricing, rather than an anticipatory charge per user per seat per month subscription basis. Perhaps for some applications, which are expensive to implement, there will be a minimum monthly usage fee in addition to set-up costs.

SaaS is here to stay and it changes our options. Now we can do our work wherever we are, accessing information and applications even when we are not at our own computing system. That, may, in fact, change what kind of computing system we need. And that might be the most profound change SaaS makes.

www.ingramcontent.com/pod-product-compliance
Lightning Source LLC
Chambersburg PA
CBHW021146070326
40689CB00044B/1150